MW00331946

Beauty and Bounty™

A CELEBRATION
OF OLYMPIC NATIONAL PARK &
OLYMPIC COAST CUISINE

Published by:

BEAUTY AND BOUNTY
2824 Sahalee Drive East
Sammamish, WA 98074
beautyandbounty@outlook.com

Printed by CreateSpace

Copyright © 2018 BEAUTY AND BOUNTY
Beauty and Bounty™ 2018

All Rights Reserved. No part of this book, including the pictures, may be reproduced or transmitted in any form or by any means whatsoever without express written permission from the publisher, except in the case of brief quotations in reviews. Please refer all pertinent questions to the publisher.

ISBN-13: 978-0692081099
ISBN-10: 0692081097

To Bart, Jane and Nick

Acknowledgments

I wish to thank the lodges, resorts, restaurants, wineries, cideries, creameries, farms and outfitters for sharing their delicious Olympic Coast Cuisine recipes as well as family and friends for sharing their favorites.

A heartfelt thank you to Jason Hoppe for your instruction and design expertise, and to Kara Phillips for editing. Publishing this book would be impossible without both of you.

Michael, thank you always for smoothing out the rough edges.

A very special thank you to the artists for capturing the beauty of Olympic National Park.

Cover, *Kalaloch, Pastel*, Barbara Benedetti Newton
Botanical Illustrations, Laska Summers
Graphic Design, Stephanie Greig

"Everybody needs beauty as well as bread, places to play in and pray in, where Nature may heal and cheer and give strength to body and soul alike.

- John Muir

CONTENTS

Spirit of the Olympics, Silkscreen, Elton Bennett

INTRODUCTION

Olympic National Park truly feels like three parks in one. Located on Washington State's Olympic Peninsula, the park encompasses rugged, snow-capped peaks, glacially carved lakes, old-growth, temperate rain forests and over 70 miles of wild coastline. The diverse and simply breathtaking wilderness is surrounded on three sides by water, and while most of the park can only be accessed by foot, one can enjoy much of the park's immense beauty by car.

The various microclimates on the Olympic Peninsula provide a rich environment for cultivating a bounty where Olympic Coast Cuisine is created. Local and seasonal fruits, vegetables, lavender, honey, fresh caught seafood, hunted game and the regions Native American heritage all lay the foundation for a unique farm to sea to table adventure. So wonderful is the food scene in and around Olympic National Park, the Olympic Culinary Loop was established. Here you will find many recipes from several outstanding venues on the Loop.

With nature at its finest, many delicious dining destinations, hand-crafted wines, ciders, cheese and stunning art, the beauty and bounty within and around the Olympic National Park is guaranteed to thrill your senses! Enjoy!

Artists are beckoned to paint the beauty and mood of Olympic National Park. Here you will find paintings by many talented and acclaimed artists.

APPETIZERS

Dungeness Crab Cakes
with Smoked Jalapeño Aioli

Baked Seastack

Razor Clam Fritters

Summer Heirloom Tomato Bruschetta

Strawberry & Brie Balsamic Flatbread

Maple Ginger Salmon Bites

Oysters Rockefeller

Baked Seafood & Hearts of Palm Dip

Twice-Baked Ozette Potatoes with
Smoked Salmon & Ikura

Hurricane Ridge, Watercolor, David McEown

Dungeness Crab Cakes with Smoked Jalapeño Aioli

Chef Ashley Miller, Creekside Restaurant, Kalaloch Lodge, Olympic National Park

Serves 8

Smoked Jalapeño Aioli

1½ cups mayonnaise

¼ cup roasted garlic, pureed

2 Jalapeño peppers, smoked and seeded

Crab Cakes

1¼ pound cooked Dungeness crabmeat

½ red bell pepper, minced

½ fresh Jalapeño pepper, minced

½ lemon, zested and juiced

2¼ teaspoons dried tarragon

½ cup mayonnaise

2 tablespoons Dijon mustard

1½ teaspoons Old Bay seasoning

1½ cups Panko breadcrumbs

Salt and freshly ground pepper to taste

2 tablespoons vegetable oil

❖ For the Smoked Jalapeño Aioli, combine all aioli ingredients in a food processor and blend until smooth. Cover and chill until serving.

❖ For the Crab Cakes, strain the crabmeat to remove and discard any liquid and possible shells. Place crabmeat into a large mixing bowl.

❖ In a medium bowl, combine all remaining ingredients except the Panko breadcrumbs, salt and pepper. Gently fold this mixture into the crabmeat.

❖ Add just enough Panko breadcrumbs to the crabmeat to bind the mixture. It should not be wet, but also not overly dry. Season to taste with salt and pepper.

❖ Shape mixture into 16 even balls, then flatten into disks to make 16 uniform cakes.

❖ Heat oil in a large skillet over medium heat. Gently fry the cakes until golden brown on both sides and heated through. Drain on paper towels and transfer to a warmed serving plate.

❖ Serve Crab Cakes with a dollop of Smoked Jalapeño Aioli.

Baked Seastack

Mt. Townsend Creamery, Port Townsend

Serves 6

Ingredients

1   **puff pastry sheet, chilled, not frozen**

1   **wheel Mt. Townsend Seastack cheese**

2   **tablespoons blackberry jam with cracked pepper or fig preserve**

❖ Preheat oven to 400°.

❖ Roll out one puff pastry sheet to ⅛-inch thick square. Transfer to a baking sheet lined with parchment paper or a ceramic baking dish.

❖ Place a wheel of Seastack cheese in the center of the dough square. Spread the jam over the top of the cheese.

❖ One corner at a time, drape the dough over the Seastack to cover it. Place in the oven and bake for 30 minutes or until the pastry is golden brown.

❖ Remove from oven and allow the cheese to rest 8 to 10 minutes before serving. For maximum gooeyness, don't wait, cut into the Seastack immediately and serve.

Razor Clam Fritters

Chef Ronald Wisner, Ocean Crest Resort, Moclips

Serves 4

Ingredients

1   pound Razor clams

1   roasted red bell pepper

1   rib of celery

½   cup grated carrots

5   ounces cream cheese

¼   cup Old Bay seasoning

2½ cups Japanese Breadcrumbs
(or Panko bread crumbs),
plus more to coat

2   eggs

❖ Place first six ingredients into a food processor and chop lightly.

❖ Place clam mixture into a large mixing bowl, add eggs and bread crumbs, and mix well by hand.

❖ Preheat a lightly oiled pan to 350°.

❖ Scoop 4-ounces of clam fritter mixture and roll in breadcrumbs to coat. Press into each patty and cook in the hot pan until golden brown on both sides.

Early on the scene, Avalanche and Glacier lilies bloom when the sunlight melts just enough snow for them to burst forth. Mid-June through mid-July is optimal for wildflower viewing on Hurricane Ridge.

Hurricane Mist, Oil, Bhavani Krishnan

Summer Heirloom Tomato Bruschetta

Serves 6

Ingredients

4   fresh, ripe, firm
    Heirloom tomatoes

4   large, fresh basil leaves

6   ½-inch-thick slices
    crusty bread

4   cloves garlic, peeled
    and mashed

    Salt and freshly
    ground pepper

3   tablespoons extra-virgin
    olive oil

❖ Halve the tomatoes lengthwise and remove as many seeds
   as possible with the tip of a knife. Dice the tomatoes into
   ¾-inch cubes.

❖ Tear the basil by hand into tiny pieces and gently stir into the
   cut tomatoes.

❖ Grill the bread on both sides. Remove from the grill and rub
   one side of each slice with the mashed garlic.

❖ Spoon the tomato and basil onto the bread, sprinkle with salt
   and pepper and top with a drizzle of olive oil. Serve warm.

Strawberry & Brie Balsamic Flatbread

Serves 4 to 6

Ingredients

2   8-inch flatbreads
8   ounces Brie cheese, rind removed and thinly sliced
1½ cups sliced, fresh strawberries
    Zest of ½ lemon
1   cup arugula
4   large basil leaves, thinly sliced
    Olive oil
    Balsamic glaze

❖ Preheat the oven to 425°. Line a baking sheet with parchment paper.

❖ Place the flatbreads on the baking sheet and brush evenly with olive oil. Bake for 2 minutes, turn over, and bake an additional 2 minutes.

❖ Remove baking sheet from the oven and set aside for flatbreads to cool slightly. Keep the oven at 425°.

❖ Meanwhile, combine strawberries in a small bowl with the lemon zest. Top the flatbreads evenly with the Brie slices and strawberries. Return to the oven for 3 to 4 minutes or until cheese melts.

❖ Remove baking sheet from oven. Top the flatbreads with arugula and basil leaves. Lightly drizzle with Balsamic glaze. Cut into pieces and serve immediately.

The breathtaking Olympic Mountains are comprised of nine towering summits named: Mount Olympus, Mount Constance, Mount Anderson, The Brothers, Mount Deception, Mount Washington, Mount Angeles, Mount Stone and Mount Ellinor.

North from Hurricane Ridge, Oil, Kathryn Townsend

Maple Ginger Salmon Bites

Serves 6

Ingredients

1   cup maple syrup

⅓   cup soy sauce

1   tablespoon grated,
    fresh ginger

24 ounces skinned salmon fillet,
    cut into bite-sized cubes

¼   cup freshly ground
    black pepper

Garnish

2   tablespoons minced
    fresh chives

❖ In a small bowl, combine maple syrup, soy sauce and ginger. Pour into a large zip-lock bag and add salmon cubes. Marinate in the refrigerate for 24 hours, turning the bag several times to coat the salmon well.

❖ Preheat oven to 500°. Line a baking sheet with parchment paper.

❖ Remove salmon cubes from marinade, discarding the marinade. Arrange salmon cubes on baking sheet and generously season with pepper.

❖ Bake salmon for 3 to 4 minutes. Remove from oven, arrange salmon on a warm serving platter and garnish with minced chives. Serve immediately with tooth picks.

Abundant and pristine snowfall graces Hurricane Ridge, about 400-feet annually, creating a winter wonderland for artists' muse and visitors' play.

Oysters Rockefeller

Compliments of Wind Rose Winery, Sequim

Makes 12

Ingredients
1 dozen mid-size oysters
4 slices of bacon
   Cocktail or Sriracha sauce
   Parmesan cheese

❖ Put oven rack on the highest position. Set oven to broil on high.

❖ Shuck and clean oysters. Detach from shell. On each oyster, spoon ½ teaspoon of cocktail sauce, then ¼ slice of bacon, followed by a generous pinch of Parmesan cheese.

❖ Place oysters in a large baking dish. Broil 6 oysters at a time, keeping the oven door cracked open. Broil for 5 minutes or until bacon begins to brown.

❖ Remove and serve hot.

❖ Best served with Wind Rose Cellars 2012 Rosato or 2012 Pinot Grigio.

Hurricane Ridge is named after its hurricane-force winds, which historically gust above 80 miles per hour. The winds, combined with blowing snow and ice, create a force to reckon with at times.

Baked Seafood & Hearts of Palm Dip

Serves 6

Ingredients

½ cup cream cheese, room temperature

¼ cup mayonnaise

⅛ teaspoon Cayenne pepper

1 14-ounce can Hearts of Palm, drained and chopped

¾ cup cooked Dungeness crabmeat

¼ cup Bay shrimp

2 tablespoons minced green onion

1 garlic clove, minced

½ cup freshly grated Parmesan cheese, plus 2 tablespoons

Salt and freshly ground pepper

Baguette slices

❖ Preheat oven to 350°.

❖ In a large bowl, beat the cream cheese with an electric mixer until smooth. Mix in mayonnaise and Cayenne. Fold in Hearts of Palm, crabmeat, shrimp, onion, garlic and ½ cup Parmesan cheese. Season with salt and pepper to taste.

❖ Transfer the mixture to an oven-to-table baking dish and bake for 15 minutes. Remove from oven and sprinkle with the remaining 2 tablespoons Parmesan cheese and continue baking until dip is bubbling and the top is golden brown.

❖ Serve the dip with crusty baguette slices.

Twice-Baked Ozette Potatoes with Smoked Salmon & Ikura

Compliments of the Washington State Potato Commission

Serves 6

Ingredients

6	medium Ozette potatoes
	Olive oil
	Sea salt
3	tablespoons Mascarpone cheese
3	tablespoons diced, cold smoked salmon
2	tablespoons chopped chives
	Freshly ground white pepper

Garnish

1	ounce Ikura (preserved salmon roe)
	Chive tips

❖ Preheat oven to 375°.

❖ Toss the potatoes with olive oil and sea salt to taste. Bake until tender, about 20 minutes.

❖ Split potatoes in half lengthwise. Scoop out the centers of each being careful not to damage the skin. With a fork, combine and mash the potato centers with Mascarpone cheese, salmon and chives. Season to taste with Sea salt and pepper.

❖ Fill potato halves with filling and bake until light golden brown, about 12 to 15 minutes.

❖ Garnish each potato with ½ teaspoon Ikura and chive tips. Serve immediately.

The sparkling Elwah River flows straight from the heart of the Olympic Mountains. Fall is a perfect time to take in the Elwah River Valley's colorful foliage.

Elwah River, Digital Art, Laska Summers

SOUPS & CHOWDERS

Clam Chowder

Roasted Pumpkin Soup

Dungeness Crab & Chermoula Soup

Creamy Cauliflower & Saffron Soup

Seafood Bisque

Spot Prawn Gazpacho

Curried Oyster Stew

Honey Ginger Carrot Soup

Smoked Salmon Chowder

Lake Crescent Lodge, Watercolor Drawing, Andrew Wicklund

Clam Chowder

Chef Ashley Miller, Creekside Restaurant, Kalaloch Lodge, Olympic National Park
Serves 4 to 6

Ingredients

6   cups milk
4   Yukon Gold potatoes, cut into 1-inch cubes
½   bay leaf
4⅓ cups clam juice
¾   pounds bacon, diced
1¾ cups diced yellow onion
¾   cups diced celery
¼   cup garlic cloves, minced
¼   cup dry sherry wine
    Clarified butter, as needed
6   tablespoons all-purpose flour
3   teaspoons fresh thyme, minced
1¼ pounds raw, chopped surf clams
½   ounce clam base
    Freshly ground pepper to taste

❖ In a large pot over medium heat, combine milk, potatoes, bay leaf and clam juice.

❖ In a large skillet, cook the bacon on low until fat is rendered and bacon is crispy. Remove bacon from the skillet and set aside. Reserve the drippings in a separate container.

❖ Into the same large skillet (without adding more fat), add the onion, celery and garlic. Sauté on low heat until the vegetables are soft.

❖ Add sherry wine to the same large skillet and over medium heat, deglaze and reduce the liquid to less than half.

❖ Measure the reserved bacon drippings and, if needed, add enough clarified butter to equal a total of ¾ cup of drippings.

❖ In a separate skillet, heat the drippings on low heat. Add flour to make a roux and cook for 5 minutes.

❖ Add the milk/potato mixture to the sautéed vegetables and bring to a boil. Slowly whisk in the roux and reduce heat to a simmer.

❖ Add the bacon, fresh thyme, bay leaf, clams and clam base. Simmer for 30 minutes.

❖ Season with pepper to taste. Remove and discard bay leaf.

❖ Ladle chowder into soup bowls and serve.

Roasted Pumpkin Soup

Michael's Seafood & Steakhouse, Port Angeles

Serves 4

Ingredients

1   2-pound fresh,
    Sugar pumpkin
1   small yellow onion,
    thinly sliced
1   tablespoon garlic, minced
6   ounces unsalted butter
1   tablespoon mild curry powder
1   teaspoon cinnamon
½   teaspoon nutmeg
½   teaspoon allspice
1   cup dry sherry
4   cups chicken stock
½   cup honey
2   cups heavy cream
    Dash of Worcestershire sauce
8   fresh sage leaves
    Salt and freshly ground pepper

❖ Preheat oven to 375°.

❖ Halve the pumpkin and remove seeds. Place cut side down on a baking sheet and roast until soft to the touch. Chill pumpkin in the refrigerator until cool enough to handle. Remove skin and cut into chunks.

❖ In a heavy bottom, 1 gallon pot, melt the butter. Add onions and garlic, cook until soft. Add the spices and cook 5 more minutes.

❖ Deglaze the pan with the sherry and cook for another 5 minutes. Add the roasted pumpkin and remaining ingredients. Simmer for 30 minutes. Allow to cool slightly and puree with a hand held immersion blender or carefully in a food processor.

❖ Season to taste with salt and pepper, if needed. If the soup is too thick, add a bit of water to thin. Ladle into soup bowls and serve.

Lake Crescent Lodge was built in 1915 and originally called Singer's Lake Crescent Tavern. The historic resort is situated in an old-growth forest on the shores of serene Lake Crescent.

Dungeness Crab & Chermoula Soup

Chef Jess Owen, Ocean Crest Resort, Moclips

Serves 6

Ingredients

½ pound diced onion

¼ pound diced carrot

¼ pound diced celery

½ cup, plus 1 tablespoon vegetable oil

Pinch of Salt

1 tablespoon Chermoula spice

½ cup potato starch (or flour)

3 cups hot vegetable stock

3 cups heavy cream

¼ cup honey

1 cup Golden raisins

1 pound cooked Dungeness crabmeat

1 tablespoon fresh mint, sliced fine

Salt and freshly ground pepper

Fresh crusty bread

❖ Heat a heavy bottom pot on medium. Add 1 tablespoon vegetable oil, diced vegetables and a pinch of salt. Cook vegetables for approximately 5 minutes until tender. Add the Chermoula spice and stir to distribute evenly.

❖ Add the remaining ½ cup oil and the potato starch (or flour) and stir until there is no more dry starch. Add 1 cup of hot stock, stirring continuously to eliminate lumps, and bring to just under a boil. As it heats, the stock will thicken considerably. Add the remaining stock and stir to incorporate, heating to just under a boil again.

❖ Add the heavy cream, golden raisins and honey. Continue to heat soup to 170° to 190°. Stir in mint, season to taste with salt and pepper.

❖ Add Dungeness crabmeat and serve with fresh crusty bread.

Known for its brilliant gem-like, blue waters, Lake Crescent is considered by many to be one of the most beautiful mountain lakes in the world.

Lake Crescent, Watercolor, Jacqueline Tribble

Creamy Cauliflower & Saffron Soup

Serves 6

Ingredients

2   cups water
2   cups chicken broth
¼   teaspoon coarsely crumbled
     saffron threads
3   tablespoons butter
1   large leek, white
     and green parts, sliced
2   cloves garlic, crushed
1½ pounds cauliflower,
     cut into 1-inch pieces
¾   cup half-and-half

Garnish

1   tablespoon minced
     fresh chives

❖ In a medium pot, combine the water and chicken broth and bring to a simmer. Remove from heat and add saffron threads. Cover and let sit 20 minutes.

❖ Melt 3 tablespoons butter in a heavy medium pot over medium-low heat. Add sliced leek and sauté until very tender but not brown, about 10 minutes. Add garlic and sauté 2 more minutes. Add cauliflower pieces, stir to coat. Add the saffron infused chicken broth. Bring to simmer over high heat. Reduce heat, cover, and simmer until cauliflower pieces are tender, about 20 minutes.

❖ Puree the soup with a hand held immersion blender or carefully in batches with a food processor.

❖ Stir in half-and-half and bring to simmer. Season to taste with salt and pepper.

❖ Ladle soup into bowls. Garnish with chives and serve.

The Olympic Peninsula Dining Room at Lake Crescent Lodge offers lake front views, Pacific Northwest fare and award winning wines.

Seafood Bisque

Serves 4 to 6

Ingredients

½ cup unsalted butter

1 cup onion, chopped

½ cup celery, chopped

1 small shallot, chopped

½ cup flour

½ tablespoon sugar

¼ cup brandy

¼ cup dry sherry

1 tablespoon tomato paste

½ tablespoon paprika

½ teaspoon salt

½ teaspoon pepper

¼ teaspoon Cayenne pepper

½ cup heavy cream

6 cups fish stock

8 ounces cooked
   Dungeness crabmeat

8 ounces cooked Bay shrimp

4 ounces cooked salmon

2 tablespoons cornstarch mixed
   with 1-tablespoon water
   (corn starch slurry)

❖ Heat butter in a large pot over medium-high, heat. Add the onions, celery, shallots. Sauté for 8 minutes or until tender.

❖ Add flour and sugar and cook for 10 minutes, stirring occasionally.

❖ Add brandy and cook 5 minutes. Add sherry, tomato paste, paprika, salt, pepper, Cayenne, cream and stock, and continue simmering for 15 minutes.

❖ If bisque is not thick enough, slowly add some of the cornstarch slurry, stirring constantly until thickened to your liking.

❖ Ladle bisque into serving bowls and top each bowl with equal amounts of crabmeat, shrimp and salmon.

Log Cabin Resort, Pastel, Barbara Benedetti Newton

Spot Prawn Gazpacho

Serves 4

Ingredients

1 English cucumber,
   peeled and chopped
1 red bell pepper,
   cored, seeded and chopped
4 plum tomatoes, chopped
1 red onion, chopped
3 garlic cloves, minced
3 cups tomato juice
¼ cup white Balsamic vinegar
¼ cup extra-virgin olive oil
½ tablespoon Kosher salt
1 teaspoon freshly
   ground pepper
12 Spot prawns, rinsed,
   shelled and deveined,
   remove tails
2 tablespoons fresh
   basil leaves, minced

❖ Add the first 5 ingredients to a food processor and pulsate until coarsely chopped.

❖ In a large bowl, combine the tomato juice, vinegar, olive oil, salt and pepper. Add the chopped vegetables and mix well. Chill for at least 4 to 6 hours.

❖ Meanwhile, preheat a grill pan to medium-high. Season prawns with salt and pepper. Grill about 1 to 2 minutes per side, until they are just done.

❖ Ladle the Gazpacho into individual soup bowls, top each serving with 3 prawns and sprinkle with fresh basil. Serve.

Log Cabin Resort tucked in old-growth cedars and firs, is a rustic retreat on the northern shore of Lake Crescent. Here you will find casual lakeside dining and exceptional views at the Sunnyside Cafe.

Curried Oyster Stew

Compliments of the Hamma Hamma Oyster Company, Lilliwaup

Serves 6

Ingredients

1   large carrot
1   medium onion
2   to 3 potatoes, peeled
1   quart chicken stock
1   pint oysters, drained
1   teaspoon curry powder
    (or to taste)
1   teaspoon ground cumin
    (or to taste)
1   can unsweetened coconut milk
    Salt and freshly
    ground pepper

❖ Chop the vegetables largely and simmer in chicken stock until almost tender.

❖ Add oysters and season with curry, cumin, salt and pepper. Bring back to a simmer, and cook until the oysters' edges curl and they are plump and firm. (Depending on the size of the oysters, you may want to halve them.)

❖ Add coconut milk. Reheat but don't boil. Taste for flavor and add more seasoning if necessary.

❖ Serve with crusty fresh bread or serve over rice.

Honey Ginger Carrot Soup

Serves 6

Ingredients

1   tablespoon butter

1   small Walla Walla onion
    (or other sweet onion)
    chopped

5   cups carrots, peeled
    and chopped

1   tablespoon fresh ginger, minced

2   cloves garlic, minced

4   cups chicken stock

1   tablespoon lemon juice

1   tablespoon honey

½   cup Greek yogurt

❖ In a large pot, melt butter on medium-high heat. Add onions and sauté until tender, about 8 minutes. Add carrots and ginger and sauté 2 minutes. Add garlic and sauté 1 more minute.

❖ Add chicken stock and simmer until carrots are tender, about 20 minutes.

❖ Puree the soup with a hand held immersion blender or carefully in batches with a food processor. Stir in lemon juice.

❖ In a small bowl combine the honey and Greek yogurt. Ladle the soup into individual serving bowls and serve each with a dollop of honey-yogurt.

The scenic Spruce Railway Trail winds along the shores of Lake Crescent. A popular, 8-mile round trip hike, the path follows an old railroad once used to haul Sitka spruce trees out of the surrounding forest.

Smoked Salmon Chowder

Serves 4

Ingredients

3   tablespoons butter

1   pound red potatoes, scrubbed
    and cut into ½-inch cubes

1   medium yellow onion, minced

2   large celery ribs, minced

2   cloves garlic, minced

¼   cup all-purpose flour

⅛   teaspoon Cayenne pepper

1   cup chicken broth

2   cups milk

1   cup heavy cream

1   teaspoon minced, fresh dill

1   Bay leaf

12 ounces smoked salmon,
    cut into ½-inch pieces

2   tablespoons chopped
    fresh Italian parsley

❖ In a large pot, melt the butter over medium heat and add the potatoes, onion, celery and sauté for 5 minutes. Add the garlic and cook 1 minute.

❖ Whisk the flour and Cayenne pepper into the vegetables and cook for 1 minute. Slowly whisk in the broth, milk, heavy cream and dill and bring to a boil, then reduce to a simmer. Add the Bay leaf and simmer until the potatoes are tender, stirring occasionally.

❖ Remove and discard the Bay leaf. Gently stir in the smoked salmon.

❖ Ladle the chowder into soup bowls and garnish each with chopped parsley and serve.

A short distance from Lake Crescent Lodge, visitors can hike to the breathtaking Marymere Falls, named in honor of Mary Alice Barnes, the sister of Charles Barnes, a member of the Press Expedition and homesteader along the shores of Lake Crescent.

Abundance at Marymere, Oil, Sandy Byers

SALADS

Spinach Blackberry Salad with Maple Vinaigrette

Autumn Roasted Beet, Carrot & Red Onion Salad

Flank Steak Salad with Mystery Bay Chèvre

Sweet, Tart & Spicy Shrimp Salad

Red Potato Salad with Dill

Dungeness Crab Salad on Butter Lettuce

Warm Mushroom, Bacon & Spinach Salad

Grilled Shrimp Caesar Salad

Moscato Poached Pear Salad

Sol Duc Rapids, Oil, Mark Boyle

Spinach Blackberry Salad with Maple Vinaigrette

Chef Ashley Miller, Creekside Restaurant, Kalaloch Lodge, Olympic National Park

Serves 4

Maple Vinaigrette Dressing

½ cup white Balsamic vinegar
1¼ cups olive oil
⅛ cup Pure maple syrup
1½ teaspoons Dijon mustard
    Salt and freshly ground pepper

Pickled Red Onion

2 small red onions, julienned
1 cup apple cider vinegar
1 cup water
⅛ cup sugar
¼ teaspoon salt
⅛ cup pickling spices in a sachet

Salad

16 ounces of fresh baby spinach
4 ounces fresh blackberries
4 ounces Feta cheese, crumbled
4 ounces Maple Vinaigrette Dressing

❖ For the Maple Vinaigrette Dressing, in a blender, add all ingredients except olive oil and blend until smooth. Gently stream the oil into the blender until fully incorporated. Season with salt and pepper to taste.

❖ For the Pickled Red Onion, place all ingredients except onions into a non-reactive (stainless steel) pan. Bring to a boil and add the onions. Boil for one minute then remove from heat. Pour mixture with liquid into a 9 x 13 glass dish to cool. Once cool, strain liquid and reserve onions.

❖ In a medium bowl, toss the baby spinach with the Maple Vinaigrette Dressing then divide among 4 salad plates. Garnish with blackberries, Feta cheese and Picked Red Onions.

Autumn Roasted Beet, Carrot & Red Onion Salad

Chef Steve Corson, Camaraderie Cellars, Port Angeles

Serves 6

Ingredients

6 to 8 medium beets, peeled and cut into 1-inch pieces

4 medium carrots, peeled and cut into 1-inch diagonal pieces

2 red onions, peeled and cut into eighths

Olive oil

Salt

Freshly ground pepper

Dressing

1 orange, zested and juiced

1 tablespoon Lemon thyme or regular thyme

Creamy goat cheese, if desired

❖ Preheat oven to 400°.

❖ Line a baking sheet with parchment paper.

❖ Toss the vegetables in oil and season with salt and pepper.

❖ Spread the vegetables out on the lined baking sheet and roast until tender and caramelized, about 30 to 45 minutes.

❖ Remove vegetables from the oven and allow to cool.

❖ Toss the cooled vegetables with the dressing ingredients and serve.

❖ If desired, top with creamy goat cheese.

Flank Steak Salad with Mystery Bay Chèvre

Compliments of Mystery Bay Farm, Marrowstone Island

Serves 4 to 6

Ingredients

1   2-pound Flank steak

¼   cup extra-virgin olive oil

2   cups field greens per serving

8   to 12 ounces Mystery Bay Chèvre with Chives, cut into ¼-inch thick slices

Sea salt

Freshly ground pepper

❖ Marinate the Flank steak in olive oil, sea salt and pepper for at least 15 minutes. Meanwhile, prepare a grill.

❖ Grill the Flank steak to your liking. Remove from grill and slice diagonally, across the grain into ¼ to ½-inch thick slices.

❖ Place the field greens onto 4 to 6 plates. Divide the strips of grilled steak on each bed of greens, and top with 2 rounds each of sliced Mystery Bay Chèvre with Chives.

❖ Serve and enjoy!

Sol Duc Hot Springs Resort provides rustic cabins, a campground, three mineral hot spring soaking pools and one freshwater pool. Relax with a poolside Swedish massage and enjoy Northwest cuisine in the Springs Restaurant.

Sol Duc Hot Springs, Acrylic, Elizabeth Henderson

Sweet, Tart & Spicy Shrimp Salad

From the Kitchen of Ronny Chirman

Serves 4

Dressing

¼ cup freshly squeezed lime juice

3 tablespoons golden brown sugar

2 tablespoons fish sauce

2 tablespoons vegetable oil

1 tablespoon finely grated lime peel

1 teaspoon hot chili paste

1 teaspoon peeled and grated fresh ginger

Salad

2 pounds English cucumbers

1½ teaspoons salt

1 tablespoon vegetable oil

¾ cup lightly roasted peanuts

1 pound cooked medium shrimp

4 cups thinly sliced Napa cabbage

3 green onion strips, minced

1 large red bell cut into thin strips

½ cup fresh cilantro

½ cup torn basil leaves

2 teaspoons black sesame seeds, toasted

❖ For Dressing, whisk together all Dressing ingredients in a small bowl. Set aside.

❖ Peel half of the cucumbers. Halve all of the cucumbers lengthwise. Scoop out the seeds with a small spoon. Cut cumbers horizontally into ¼-inch thick slices. Place the slices into a colander and let drain for 30 minutes.

❖ Heat 1 tablespoon vegetable oil in a large skillet. Add the peanuts and sauté until golden.

❖ In a large bowl combine the shrimp, cabbage, bell pepper, green onion, cilantro and basil.

❖ Pat cucumber pieces dry and add to salad. Toss with Dressing, sprinkle with peanuts and black sesame seeds and serve.

Red Potato Salad with Dill

Compliments of Westport Winery Garden Resort, Westport

Serves 4 to 6

Ingredients

2 pounds small red potatoes, quartered

12 eggs, hard-cooked and sliced

2 stalks celery, diced

½ cup diced red onion

8 spears diced dill pickle

1 cup mayonnaise

1 cup sour cream

1 tablespoon Champagne vinegar

1 tablespoon Dijon mustard

2 tablespoons fresh dill

½ tablespoon salt

⅛ teaspoon freshly ground pepper

2 tablespoons sugar

❖ In a large pot, cover potatoes with water, bring to a boil and continue boiling for about 10 to 12 minutes, until just tender. Pour off water, set the pot in a sink or in a larger pan of cold water to cool the potatoes quickly.

❖ In a large bowl, combine the potatoes with eggs, celery, red onion and diced dill pickle.

❖ In another bowl, combine the sour cream, mayonnaise, vinegar and Dijon mustard. Add to the potatoes and stir gently to combine. Fold in the dill and add salt and pepper and serve.

In the Quileute language, the name "Sol Duc" means "sparkling waters".

From the Source, Pastel, Janet Hamilton

Dungeness Crab Salad on Butter Lettuce

Serves 4

Ingredients

1   **pound jumbo lump crabmeat, picked over to remove any shell or cartilage**

½   **cup minced fennel, core removed**

4   **teaspoons finely sliced fresh chives**

1   **teaspoon minced fresh tarragon leaves**

⅓   **cup mayonnaise**

3   **tablespoons sour cream**

1   **teaspoon freshly squeezed lemon juice**

½   **teaspoon Dijon mustard**

     Kosher salt

     Freshly ground pepper

4   **Butter lettuce leaves**

❖ In a medium bowl, gently combine the crabmeat, fennel, chives, and tarragon.

❖ In a small bowl, stir together the mayonnaise, sour cream, lemon juice and mustard. Fold into the crabmeat mixture and gently mix until combined. Season with salt and pepper to taste. Chill until ready to serve.

❖ Arrange Butter lettuce leaves on 4 plates. Top each with an equal amount of chilled Dungeness Crab Salad and serve.

The family friendly hike from the hot springs through the lush, old-growth forest will lead you to Sol Duc Falls, an inspiration for many plein air artists.

Warm Mushroom, Bacon & Spinach Salad

Serves 4

Salad

6   slices thick bacon, finely chopped

1   tablespoon olive oil

¼   red onion, sliced

1   pound Cremini mushrooms, sliced

1   clove garlic, minced
    Salt
    Freshly ground pepper

6   cups baby spinach

4   tablespoons freshly shaved Parmigiana Reggiano

Dressing

2   teaspoons Dijon mustard

2   teaspoons Pure maple syrup

¼   cup white Balsamic vinegar

½   cup extra-virgin olive oil

❖ In a large skillet, cook bacon until just crisp. Set bacon aside to drain onto paper towels. Remove all but 1 tablespoon of bacon drippings in the skillet.

❖ Add 1 tablespoon olive oil to the skillet and heat over medium-high heat. Add onions and sauté until softened, about 5 minutes. Add mushrooms, salt and pepper and continue to cook for another 3 to 4 minutes. Add garlic and sauté 1 minute longer. Turn heat to low.

❖ For the Dressing, in a small bowl combine and whisk together the mustard, maple syrup and vinegar. Slowly whisk in the oil. Season to taste with salt and pepper.

❖ In a large bowl, toss together the spinach and warm mushroom mixture until the spinach starts to wilt. Add enough Dressing to taste.

❖ Arrange the salad among 4 salad plates, top with equal amounts of crumbled bacon and Parmesan cheese shavings. Serve warm.

Grilled Shrimp Caesar Salad

Serves 4

Ingredients

1   pound raw, large shrimp, shelled and deveined, tails removed
1   teaspoon vegetable oil
¼   teaspoon Cayenne pepper
    Salt
6   Romaine lettuce leaves, torn into bite size pieces

Caesar Dressing

¼   cup mayonnaise
¼   cup fresh lemon juice
1   clove garlic, crushed
½   teaspoon anchovy paste
½   teaspoon Worcestershire sauce
¼   teaspoon Dijon mustard
¼   teaspoon freshly ground pepper
¼   cup extra-virgin olive oil

Parmesan Crisps

2   ounces Parmesan cheese, coarsely shredded

❖ In a large bowl, toss shrimp with vegetable oil, Cayenne and a dash of salt. In a grill pan over medium-high heat, cook the shrimp 2 minutes per side until done and opaque throughout. Remove shrimp from grill and let cool.

❖ For the Caesar Dressing, in a medium bowl, whisk together mayonnaise, lemon juice, garlic, anchovy paste, Worcestershire sauce and pepper until blended. Drizzle extra-virgin olive oil in a slow, steady stream while whisking until emulsified. Cover and refrigerate up to 2 days.

❖ For the Parmesan Crisps, preheat the oven to 375°. Line a baking sheet with parchment paper. Mound 1 tablespoon of grated cheese onto the baking sheet. Press each mound into 3-inch rounds and space a few inches apart. Bake 5 to 6 minutes or until light golden brown. Cool completely on the sheet over a wire rack. They can be stored in an airtight container up to 1 day.

❖ Toss the romaine with the Caesar Dressing and divide among 4 salad plates. Top each serving with Grilled Shrimp and Parmesan Crisps and serve.

Moscato Poached Pear Salad

Serves 6

Moscato Poached Pears

1   bottle Moscato wine

1   tablespoon freshly squeezed lemon juice

¼   cup honey

3   ripe Anjou or Bosc pears peeled, halved and cored

Dressing

1   teaspoon Dijon mustard

2   tablespoons white Balsamic Vinegar

6   tablespoons olive oil

1   teaspoon salt
     Freshly ground pepper

Salad

6   cups mixed salald greens

½   cup fresh blueberries

½   cup candied nuts

¾   cup Gorgonzola cheese, crumbled

❖ For the Dressing, in a small bowl whisk together the mustard and vinegar. Whisk in the olive oil, salt and pepper to taste. Set aside until ready to use.

❖ For the Moscato Poached Pears, in a small pot, add the pears and drizzle with lemon juice then honey. Pour in enough wine to cover the pears, then bring to a simmer over medium heat. Cook for 15 to 20 minutes or until the pears just become soft when pierced with a knife. Do not over cook or the pears will be become mushy. Transfer the pears to a plate to cool and discard the liquid. Cut pears into several slices.

❖ To assemble the salad, in a medium bowl, add the salad greens and toss with just enough Dressing to coat. Divide the dressed greens onto 6 salad plates. Top with equal amounts of poached pear slices, blueberries, candied nuts and Gorgonzola cheese.

During late October/November, watch nature repeat the cycle of life as the weary, but determined, Coho salmon leap over the falls on their way to spawn upstream in the Sol Duc River.

Salmon Cascades, Digital Art, Laska Summers

BREADS & BREAKFAST

Raspberry Almond Scones

Morning Crab Stacks

Monte "Cresto" Sandwich

Country Quiche

Ricotta Pancakes with Honey & Pears

Peachy Rhubarb Muffins

Smoked Salmon Scramble

Campfire Cheese Bread

Apple Buttermilk Loaves

Wild Thimbleberry Flower, Oil, Mark Boyle

Raspberry Almond Scones

Compliments of Westport Winery Garden Resort, Westport

Serves 8

Ingredients

2   cups all-purpose flour
1   tablespoon baking powder
½   cup sugar
¼   teaspoon salt
½   cup cold butter,
    cut into ½-inch dice
½   cup buttermilk
1   egg
1   teaspoon vanilla
½   cup frozen raspberries

Raspberry Almond Streusel

¼   cup butter, melted
¼   cup flour
¼   cup sugar
    Pinch salt
¼   cup sliced almonds

Glaze

1   cup powdered sugar
1   teaspoon almond extract
1   tablespoon water

❖ Preheat oven to 400°.

❖ Into a large bowl, mix together the flour, baking powder, sugar and salt.

❖ Cut the butter into the dry ingredients using a pastry cutter or your fingertips until the butter/dry mix is the size of peas.

❖ In a small bowl, mix together the buttermilk, egg and vanilla. Add to the butter/dry mix.

❖ Use a rubber spatula or both hands to mix the dough until everything is just combined. Do not over mix. Separate into two balls and pat flat.

❖ Place ½ cup frozen raspberries on the bottom layer, then add the second round of dough with a slight dome.

❖ In a small bowl, mix together the Raspberry Almond Streusel ingredients and spread over the top of the pastry.

❖ Line a baking sheet with parchment paper. Cut into 8 wedges, separate them and place on parchment. Bake for 20 minutes.

❖ Remove scones from the oven and allow to cool. In a small bowl, mix together the Glaze, drizzle over the scones and serve.

Morning Crab Stacks
Serves 4

Crab Patties

1 pound cooked
   Dungeness crabmeat
2 tablespoons mayonnaise
1 teaspoon Dijon mustard
2 teaspoons lemon juice
¼ teaspoon dried thyme
¼ teaspoon salt
¼ teaspoon freshly ground pepper
2 celery ribs, minced
¼ cup minced red onion
½ sleeve of Saltine crackers,
   finely crushed
1 cup Panko breadcrumbs
2 tablespoons vegetable oil
4 large tomato slices

Easy Hollandaise Sauce

½ cup sour cream
½ cup mayonnaise
2 teaspoons lemon juice
1 teaspoon yellow mustard

Poached Eggs

4 eggs
4 Butter lettuce leaves
   Fresh, minced chives

❖ For the Crab Patties, in a large bowl, combine all ingredients except: Saltine crackers, Panko breadcrumbs, oil and tomato slices.

❖ Slowly add the Saltine crackers and mix well. If the mixture is too wet to mold into a patty, add more crackers; if it's too dry, add a bit more mayonnaise. Divide the mixture into 4 patties, using a small ring mold or round cookie cutter.

❖ Spread the Panko breadcrumbs onto a plate and press both sides of each patty into the breadcrumbs. Chill the Crab Patties for at least 30 minutes. When ready, heat 2 tablespoons oil in a medium non-stick skillet over medium heat. Add the chilled patties and cook until golden brown on each side and heated through.

❖ For the Hollandaise Sauce, in a small saucepan over low heat, combine all ingredients. Cook and stir on low heat until sauce is hot.

❖ For the Poached Eggs, lightly grease a medium skillet with oil. Fill the skillet half way with water and bring to a boil. Reduce heat to a simmer. Break one egg into a measuring cup and carefully slide it into the simmering water. Repeat with the other 3 eggs. Simmer for 3 to 5 minutes or until the whites are set and the yolks begin to thicken. With a slotted spoon, transfer eggs to a plate. Season with salt and pepper.

❖ To assemble the Crab Stacks, on 4 individual plates, lay a Butter lettuce leaf, top with tomato slice, then top with a Crab Patty followed by a poached egg. Season with salt and pepper. Spoon the Hollandaise Sauce over each serving. Garnish with minced chives and serve.

Monte "Cresto" Sandwich

Chef Jess Owen, Ocean Crest Resort, Moclips

Makes 4 Sandwiches

Ingredients

8   slices French bread
3   eggs
1   cup milk
1   tablespoon vanilla extract
     Zest from ½ an orange
4   ounces thinly sliced ham
4   ounces smoked salmon
8   slices Cheddar cheese
     Powdered sugar
     Raspberry jam

❖ For the egg batter, whisk eggs, milk, vanilla, cinnamon and orange zest together.

❖ For the sandwiches, dip the bread slices in the egg batter and make French Toast as normal.

❖ Heat the ham, turkey and smoked salmon in a large pan or on a griddle. Melt the Cheddar cheese on the French Toast slices and build 4 Monte Cresto sandwiches by adding turkey, ham and smoked salmon.

❖ Plate the Monte Cresto sandwiches and dust each with powdered sugar. Serve with raspberry jam.

The Sol Duc River and other tributaries of the Quillayute River carry some the most abundant stock of wild winter steelhead in the Pacific Northwest. Sol Duc River sustains all five major species of salmon.

River Bend, Watercolor, Roy Lowry

Country Quiche

Compliments of Westport Winery Garden Resort, Westport

Makes 2, 10-Inch Quiches

Ingredients

2   pounds sweet sausage

2   sprigs rosemary

3   cups potatoes, peeled
    and thinly sliced

1   red onion, chopped

2   unbaked 10-inch pie shells

12 slices Cheddar cheese

3   cups heavy cream

12 eggs

❖ Preheat oven to 350°.

❖ In large skillet, cook and crumble the sweet sausage.

❖ Add rosemary sprigs, potatoes and onion and sauté for 5 minutes. Remove and discard the sprigs.

❖ Divide the sausage mixture between the 2 pie shells. Top each with 6 slices of cheese.

❖ In a large bowl, blend together the cream and eggs. Pour into the pie crusts over the cheese in each pie shell.

❖ Bake the quiche for 55 minutes. Serve warm or at room temperature.

Ricotta Pancakes with Honey & Pears

Serves 6

Honey Pear Topping

3   tablespoons unsalted butter
¼   cup honey
2   medium pears, cored, peeled and cut into ½-inch cubes
½   teaspoon ground cinnamon
1   teaspoon vanilla extract

Ricotta Pancakes

1   cup Ricotta cheese, drained of excess liquid
1   cup sour cream
3   eggs, separated
½   teaspoon baking soda
1   cup all-purpose flour
    Dash salt
1   tablespoon sugar
2   tablespoons lemon juice

❖ In a small skillet over medium heat, melt butter. Add brown sugar and cook until butter has melted and sugar has dissolved. Add pears, cinnamon and vanilla and cook, stirring occasionally, for 10 minutes. Remove from heat.

❖ In a medium bowl, beat together the Ricotta, sour cream and egg yolks.

❖ In a small bowl, combine baking soda, flour, salt and sugar.

❖ In another small bowl, beat the egg whites until fluffy.

❖ Heat a griddle or non-stick skillet over medium-low heat.

❖ Stir the flour mixture into the Ricotta mixture, blending well but do not beat. Stir in lemon juice, then gently fold in beaten egg whites.

❖ Add 1 tablespoon butter to the griddle to coat surface. When hot, pour a small amount of batter (approximately ¼ cup) into pan, spread out with a spoon.

❖ When bubbles appear on the surface and begin to break, turn over and cook the other side until golden light brown.

❖ Serve the Ricotta Pancakes immediately with butter and Honey Pear Topping.

Hoh River Bend, Pastel, James Geddes

Peachy Rhubarb Muffins

Makes 24 muffins

Ingredients

¾ cups vegetable oil

2 large whole eggs

1 cup buttermilk

2 teaspoons vanilla extract

2 cups all-purpose flour

½ cup sugar

½ cup brown sugar

1 teaspoon baking soda

2 teaspoons baking powder

½ teaspoon cinnamon

½ teaspoon salt

2 cups fresh rhubarb,
diced small

1 whole peach,
diced small

❖ Preheat the oven to 350°. Line two muffin pans with paper liners.

❖ In a large bowl, mix together the oil, eggs, buttermilk and vanilla.

❖ In medium bowl, mix together the flour, sugars, baking soda, baking powder, cinnamon and salt.

❖ Add the dry ingredients into the bowl of wet ingredients and mix until well-blended.

❖ Fold in the rhubarb and peaches, stirring gently until combined.

❖ Spoon the mixture into the lined muffins pans.

❖ Bake for 20 minutes or until a knife inserted in the center of a muffin comes out clean.

The Hoh River is a unique, milky slate-blue color because the river is fed by glaciers on Mount Olympus. These glaciers grind rock into a fine glacial flour which turns the Hoh River this stunning color.

Smoked Salmon Scramble

Serves 6

Ingredients

12   eggs

½   cup heavy cream

    Salt and freshly ground pepper

¼   pound sliced smoked salmon, chopped into small pieces

2   ounces cream cheese, cut into small cubes

1   tablespoon jarred pimento

2   tablespoons butter

6   teaspoons fresh chives, finely chopped, and divided

❖ In a large bowl, whisk the eggs and cream together. Add 3 teaspoons of the chopped chives. Sprinkle the eggs with salt and pepper.

❖ Preheat a large nonstick skillet over medium heat. Melt butter in the pan and add eggs. Scramble the eggs gently; do not cook until dry.

❖ When eggs are almost done, but still a little wet, stir in smoked salmon, cream cheese and pimento.

❖ Remove from heat and garnish Smoked Salmon Scramble with remaining chives. Serve immediately.

The lush, green canopy in the Hoh Rain Forest is created by several species of trees. The Sitka spruce, Western hemlock, Douglas-fir, Western red cedar, Bigleaf maple, Red alder, Vine maple and Black cottonwood provide shelter for the mossy and fern-blanketed forest floor.

Campfire Cheese Bread

Makes 1 loaf

Ingredients

2   cups all-purpose flour

1   cup shredded Campfire Smoked Jack cheese, Mt. Townsend Creamery

1   teaspoon sugar

1   teaspoon baking powder

½   teaspoon baking soda

½   teaspoon salt

1   cup buttermilk

¼   cup butter, melted

2   eggs, slightly beaten

❖ Preheat oven to 350°. Lightly grease the bottom of a loaf pan.

❖ In a medium bowl, stir together the flour, cheese, sugar, baking powder, baking soda and salt. Stir in remaining ingredients just until moistened. Spread into the loaf pan.

❖ Bake 35 to 45 minutes or until golden brown and a toothpick inserted in center comes out clean. Cool 5 minutes, then run knife around edges of pan to loosen the loaf. Transfer the loaf to a wire rack.

❖ Cool the loaf 30 minutes before slicing.

Apple Buttermilk Loaves

Compliments of the Washington Apple Commission

Makes 2 loaves

Ingredients

3   cups flour
½   teaspoon each baking powder
    and baking soda
¼   teaspoon salt
1   cup butter or margarine
1   cup sugar
1   cup packed brown sugar
3   eggs
1   teaspoon vanilla
¾   cup buttermilk
1½ cups pared, cored
    and finely chopped
    Golden Delicious apples
½   cup nuts, chopped
1   teaspoon grated orange peel

❖ Preheat oven to 350°. Grease and flour two loaf pans.

❖ In a large bowl, combine flour, baking powder, soda and salt. Set aside.

❖ In a large bowl, cream the butter and sugars. Beat in eggs one at a time and vanilla. Stir in buttermilk, alternating with some of the flour mixture. Fold in apples, nuts and orange peel.

❖ Pour batter into the prepared loaf pans.

❖ Bake 50 to 60 minutes or until wooden pick inserted near center comes out clean.

❖ Cool in pan 10 minutes, then remove loaves from pan and cool completely on a wire rack.

❖ Wrap in foil or plastic and let loaves stand overnight, allowing flavors to blend.

The Hoh Rain Forest receives the most precipitation of anywhere in the continental United States, nearly 140 to 170 inches annually.

Skunk Cabbage Reflections, Watercolor, Roy Lowry

SEAFOOD

Halibut & Roasted Leek Mashed Potatoes
with Saffron Pernod Cream Sauce

Clam Pasta with Chorizo

Cedar Planked Salmon Topped with Dungeness Crab

Salmon au Poivre with Maple Balsamic Glazed Strawberries
& White Chocolate Whipped Potatoes

Hamma Hamma Fried Oysters

Shrimp & Campfire Grits

Sautéed Sea Scallops with Garlic & Fresh Dill

Rainbow Trout with Hazelnut Butter

Baked Sole Over Asparagus Tips

Kalaloch Lodge, Watercolor, Shirley Mercer

Halibut & Roasted Leek Mashed Potatoes with Saffron Pernod Cream Sauce

Chef Ashley Miller, Creekside Restaurant, Kalaloch Lodge, Olympic National Park

Serves 4

Roasted Leek Mashed Potatoes

½ **pound leeks, white and light green parts only**

5 **pounds Yukon Gold Potatoes, peeled and quartered**

4 **tablespoons butter**

2½ **cups milk**
  Salt and freshly ground pepper to taste

Saffron Pernod Cream Sauce

2 **shallots, minced**

2 **tablespoons butter**

1 **pinch saffron threads**

¼ **cup Pernod**

2 **cups heavy cream**
  Salt and freshly ground pepper to taste

Halibut

4 **6-ounce halibut fillets, skinned and deboned**

2 **tablespoons olive oil**

❖ Preheat oven to 350°.

❖ For the Roasted Leek Mashed Potatoes, cut the leeks in half lengthwise, coat with olive oil and wrap in aluminum foil. Set wrapped leeks in the oven and roast for 30 minutes. Remove from oven and dice. Set aside 4 teaspoons for garnish. Keep the oven set at 350°. In a large pot, add potatoes and enough water to cover. Lightly salt and bring to a boil, and cook potatoes until tender and flaky. Meanwhile, in a small pot, heat the butter and milk. When the potatoes are done, strain out the water, add the milk mixture and roasted leeks. With a mixer, beat on medium speed until smooth and creamy. Season with salt and pepper.

❖ For the Saffron Pernod Cream Sauce, in a ramekin, soak the saffron threads in the Pernod and set aside.

❖ In a small heavy bottom pot, melt the butter, add the shallots and sauté over medium heat until soft. Add the saffron with Pernod and deglaze, reducing by half. Add the heavy cream and continue cooking until reduced by half. (If needed, add a bit of cornstarch slurry (one tablespoon cornstarch to 2 tablespoons cold water.)

❖ For the Halibut, in a sauté pan that is oven-safe, heat olive oil over medium-high heat, sear fillets for about 3 minutes on each side. Transfer the pan to the oven and finish cooking for another 5 to 6 minutes. To serve, divide potatoes among each plate, top with halibut and drizzle with Saffron Pernod Cream Sauce.

❖ Garnish each serving with reserved crispy leeks.

Clam Pasta with Chorizo

Compliments of Hamma Hamma Oyster Company, Lilliwaup

Serves 4

Ingredients

Butter or oil

4 pounds clams
(1 pound per person)

A few splashes dry
white wine (Sauvignon Blanc
or Muscadet work well)

1 onion, diced

1 red pepper, diced

1 clove garlic, minced

4 ounces Olympic Provisions
chorizo, thinly sliced into
rounds

Freshly ground pepper

1 teaspoon red pepper flakes,
or to taste

1 teaspoon fresh
thyme leaves,
or to taste

2 handfuls fresh arugula,
stems removed

Parmesan or Asiago
cheese, grated

❖ Rinse clams carefully in fresh water, agitating them to ensure they are all tightly closed.

❖ Add several splashes of white wine and a pat of butter to a large pot. Add the clams, cover and steam for 5 to 7 minutes. If the clams were all alive and fresh when you put them in the pot, do not worry about discarding ones that have not opened, simply cook them a bit longer. As you remove the clams, separate the meat from the shells, saving a few shells for atmosphere if you like. Reserve the meat and the broth.

❖ Sauté diced onion and red pepper in butter or olive oil until soft. Add minced garlic and sauté for a bit. Add the chorizo, and cook until the chorizo is warmed through, then add the reserved clam steaming liquid (making sure not to add any grit from the bottom of the pot). Simmer until liquid is reduced, adding black pepper, red pepper and thyme to taste.

❖ Add clams and a handful or two of the arugula, cook just until the arugula is wilted. Spoon over pasta, then sprinkle with cheese.

In the Quinault language, Kalaloch, means a "good place to land."

Cedar Planked Salmon Topped with Dungeness Crab

Chef Steve W. Little, Dockside Grill on Sequim Bay

Serves 2

For the Salmon

2 6 ounce fresh King salmon
   fillets (boneless)

1 ounce of your favorite BBQ rub

4 ounces fresh Dungeness Crab
   (claw meat)

Zucchini Provencal

1 large zucchini in 1-inch cubes

½ red onion, julienned

½ red bell pepper, julienned

½ yellow bell pepper, julienned

6 spears of asparagus, 1-inch pieces

1 teaspoon minced, fresh garlic

1 tablespoon extra-virgin olive oil
   Salt and freshly ground pepper
   to taste

Beurre Blanc

⅓ cup of your favorite white wine

½ of 1 lemon, 1 lime
   and 1 orange, juiced

½ teaspoon fresh chopped shallots

½ cup of heavy cream

4 ounces of salted butter
   Salt and white pepper to taste

❖ Preheat oven to 450°. Rub a cedar plank with a light coating of canola oil and place in oven for 5 to 10 minutes to season. Pull out and cool to room temperature. Meanwhile prepare vegetables.

❖ For the Zucchini Provencal, put all ingredients in a mixing bowl and toss together. Divide in half and pile in the center of each cedar plank.

❖ Rub the salmon fillets with extra-virgin olive oil and BBQ rub. Place the salmon halfway on the plank and halfway on the vegetables (this allows the salmon and vegetables to cook evenly).

❖ For the Beurre Blanc, in medium saucepan, whisk together shallots, wine, citrus juice, cream, salt and white pepper. On medium-high heat, bring to a boil and reduce by half. Turn to a very low heat and whisk in butter, one pat at a time until incorporated.

❖ Place the planks in the oven and cook for 15 minutes or to desired temperature for salmon.

❖ Meanwhile, melt 2 teaspoons butter in a sauté pan and add fresh Dungeness Crab.

❖ When salmon is done, heat crab just enough to heat through. Place half of the crab on each of the salmon and ladle desired amount of Beurre Blanc over the top. Serve.

The Driftwood Fire, Silkscreen, Elton Bennett

Salmon au Poivre with Maple Balsamic Glazed Strawberries & Chocolate Whipped Potatoes

Chef Jess Owen, Ocean Crest Resort, Moclips

Serves 4

Ingredients

4 ounces Pure maple syrup

4 ounces Balsamic vinegar

4 6 to 8 ounce wild salmon fillets, skinned

Olive oil spray

Salt and freshly ground pepper

6 strawberries, sliced

1 pound Yukon Gold potatoes, peeled

½ ounce Nestlé white chocolate chips

¼ teaspoon salt

2 dashes Tabasco sauce

½ cup heavy cream

❖ For the potatoes, cut them into 2-inch rounds and steam until tender when pierced with a fork, about 20 minutes.

❖ Place the potatoes in a stand mixer with wire whip attachment. Add the white chocolate chips to the still hot potatoes; mix until the chocolate starts to melt. Mix in the salt and Tabasco sauce. Pour in the heavy cream and continue mixing at low to medium speed until potatoes are creamy, about 1 minute.

❖ For the salmon and strawberries, preheat grill to medium high. Mix maple syrup with Balsamic vinegar in a pot and place on medium heat and reduce by half. When sauce is reduced, remove from heat and add sliced strawberries and set aside.

❖ Spray flesh side of salmon with olive oil, season with salt and pepper, and place on the heated grill skin side up. Grill for approximately 5 minutes. While on the grill, spray skin side of salmon with olive oil and season. Grill for approximately 3 minutes (cooking times depend on thickness of cut as well as temperature of the grill and desired doneness).

❖ Remove salmon from grill and arrange on individual plates. Serve strawberries and sauce on top of each salmon.

Hamma Hamma Fried Oysters

Compliments of Hamma Hamma Oyster Company, Lilliwaup

Serves 4

Ingredients

24 **shucked oysters
(we recommend extra-small,
small, or medium)**

   Breading (see instructions)

   Oil for frying

   Lemon wedges

   Tartar sauce

   Hot sauce

   **All of the above
   are available at Hamma
   Hamma Oyster Company**

❖ Put the oysters in a pot of water and bring the water to a boil. Once it boils, remove pot from heat and drain the oysters in a colander. Rinse them with water just so they are cool to the touch. Do not pat them dry as a little moisture is necessary for the breading to stick.

❖ Roll the oysters in your favorite flour-based seafood breading. (We highly recommend our own house made "Hall's Original" breading mix.) If you're using a Panko or other crusty breading, you'll need to be a little more careful with how you bread the oysters, and should probably roll the oysters in flour and then dunk them in an egg wash (beaten egg plus a tablespoon of water or milk) before rolling them in the Panko. Or you can add wheat flour and cornmeal to the Panko until it looks like something that will stick without a wash.

❖ Put the breaded oysters on a plate and let them sit in a refrigerator for at least 20 minutes. Then, pan fry them in a high-heat oil until they're crispy and hot. (But if olive oil is all you have, don't fret. It'll be yummy). Serve with lemon wedges, tartar, and hot sauce.

Kalaloch Cabin Number Three, Oil, Mark Boyle

Shrimp & Campfire Grits

Compliments of Mt. Townsend Creamery, Port Townsend

Serves 4

Ingredients

1   **cup grits**

4   **cups water or stock**

¼   **pound of Campfire Smoked Jack cheese, Mt. Townsend Creamery**

1   **pound medium size shrimp, peeled and deveined**

¼   **cup scallions, thinly sliced**

     Salt

     Freshly ground pepper

     Butter or oil

Garnish

     Scallions, minced

❖ In a large pot, bring the water or stock to a boil. Stir in grits, reduce heat and simmer, stirring occasionally until cooked (about 40 minutes).

❖ Grate Campfire cheese on large holes of box grater. Set aside.

❖ Season the shrimp with salt and pepper. Heat the butter or oil in a medium skillet, add the shrimp and sauté until done, about 2 minutes per side.

❖ When the grits are ready, stir in the Campfire cheese until melted.

❖ Portion the grits between 4 bowls. Serve the shrimp over the grits with a green vegetable, such as spinach or asparagus. Garnish with scallions.

The charming and historic Kalaloch Lodge and cozy cabins rest on a bluff where Kalaloch Creek flows into the driftwood-laden beaches below. It is the only Pacific coast lodge in Olympic National Park. Dine in Kalaloch's Creekside Restaurant with fresh, local fare alongside breathtaking ocean views.

Sautéed Sea Scallops with Garlic & Fresh Dill

Serves 4

Ingredients

20 very large Sea scallops
    Salt
3   tablespoons vegetable oil
¾ cup mayonnaise
3   large cloves garlic, crushed
1   tablespoon freshly squeezed
    lemon juice
1   tablespoon lemon zest
1   tablespoon minced, fresh dill
    Pinch Cayenne pepper
    Salt and freshly ground pepper
    to taste

Garnish

4   sprigs of dill

❖ In a medium bowl, combine all ingredients except the scallops. Season the scallops with salt.

❖ With a pastry brush, thoroughly coat both sides of the scallops with the mayonnaise mixture and set aside.

❖ In a large sauté pan, heat the oil until very hot. Add the scallops and sear them for 2 to 3 minutes per side until they are medium-rare to medium. Do not over cook.

❖ Remove the scallops from the pan and divide among 4 plates. Garnish with sprigs of dill.

Within a short walk from Kalaloch Lodge are several unspoiled beaches where visitors can whale watch, examine colorful tide-pools, and view the Pacific coast's unforgettable sunsets. No wonder it's been said, "Kalaloch steals a little bit of your heart."

Rainbow Trout with Hazelnut Butter

Serves 4

Hazelnut Butter

¼ cup finely
    chopped hazelnuts

1   tablespoon chopped,
    fresh Italian parsley

2   tablespoons butter, softened

2   tablespoons lemon juice

Ingredients

4   Rainbow trout fillets,
    butterflied, beheaded
    and backbones removed

    Salt and freshly
    ground pepper

1   beaten egg

½   cup milk

¼   cup all-purpose flour

¼   cup Panko breadcrumbs

¼   teaspoon salt

¼   cup vegetable oil

Garnish

    Lemon wedges

❖ For the Hazelnut Butter, microwave the hazelnuts in a shallow bowl, uncovered, on high for 30 seconds to 1 minute. Stirring once or twice, until light brown. Cool.

❖ In a small bowl, mix together the browned hazelnuts, parsley, butter and lemon juice. Set aside.

❖ Preheat the oven to 175° and set a serving platter in the oven to warm.

❖ In a shallow dish, whisk together egg and milk. In another shallow dish, mix together flour, Panko breadcrumbs and salt.

❖ Heat vegetable oil in a large skillet over medium-high heat. Season both sides of the fish with salt and pepper. In batches, coat both sides of the fillets with the flour mixture, dip into egg mixture, then back into flour mixture.

❖ Fry the fish in batches, (skin side down first) for 5 to 6 minutes on each side. Transfer cooked fillets to the platter in the warmed oven.

❖ To serve, spoon the Hazelnut Butter over the trout fillets and garnish with lemon wedges.

Baked Sole Over Asparagus Tips

Serves 4

Ingredients

1   pound asparagus, thin stalks, tough ends removed

Salt and freshly ground pepper, to taste

1   2-pound Petrale sole, cut into 4 equal portions

2   tablespoons mayonnaise

1   tablespoon finely grated lemon zest

1   tablespoon fresh squeezed lemon juice

Topping

½   cup Panko breadcrumbs

2   tablespoons melted butter

2   tablespoons finely grated Parmesan cheese

1   teaspoon minced fresh Italian parsley

❖ Preheat oven to 400°.

❖ Arrange the asparagus in a single layer in a buttered, shallow oven-to-table baking dish and season with salt and pepper. Arrange the sole on top of the asparagus and lightly season with salt and pepper.

❖ In a small bowl, combine the mayonnaise, lemon zest and juice. With a pastry brush, baste the mixture onto the sole.

❖ For the Topping, in a small bowl mix together the topping ingredients. Sprinkle evenly over the sole.

❖ Bake for 12 minutes or until sole flakes when tested with a fork.

At Kalaloch Beach, the weathered old-growth trees that long ago turned to driftwood, are as grand as the Olympic forests from which they traveled.

Kalaloch Beach, Digital Art, Laska Summers

MEATS

Shepherd's Pie

Caramelized Rib Eye Roast

Juniper Rubbed Venison Rib Chops
with Huckleberry Semi-Glace

Filet Mignon with Blue Cheese Herb Crust

Flat Iron Steak with Finnriver Habanero Cider Deglaze

Tomahawk Pork Chop with Bourbon Bacon Jam
& Wine Poached Cranberries

Cider Braised Country Style Pork Ribs

Indian Fry Bread Tacos

Leg of Lamb with Yogurt-Cucumber-Mint Sauce

Ruby Beach, Digital Art, Laska Summers

Shepherd's Pie

Chef David Lossing, Roosevelt Dining Room, Lake Quinault Lodge, Quinault

Serves 12

Ingredients

3   pounds ground elk (most butchers have a free range, organic variety if you ask)

2   pounds ground, lean, beef

2   pounds ground "Ribeye Scrap" (found at a local butcher)

1½ tablespoons Flat Leaf parsley

2   tablespoons fresh thyme

1   tablespoon dried thyme

1   large yellow onion

3   shakes Worcestershire sauce

2   tablespoons Kosher salt

1½ tablespoons black pepper

2   tablespoons minced garlic

5   cups day old mashed potatoes

1   6 to 8 ounce jar of beef gravy

1   bag of frozen vegetables (carrots, peas and corn)

¼   cup of shredded Asiago cheese

❖ Preheat to 325°.

❖ Place all the meat into a large mixing bowl.

❖ Finely chop parsley, thyme, and onion. Add to the meat and mix together, making sure everything is well incorporated.

❖ Divide the mixture between 2 large sheet pans and bake for 1 hour.

❖ Remove from oven, drain the fats and oils, using a flat spatula, chop up all the meat a bit to break it up.

❖ Place back in the oven for another 30 minutes, making sure the meat is 99% cooked through and strained.

❖ To assemble the pie, in a large, deep casserole dish layer with 2-inches of the meat mixture, then a ½-inch of the vegetables (carrots corn and peas tossed together) and a few ladle fulls of the beef gravy (about 2-ounces per ladle).

❖ Using a spoon, cover the entire pie with the mashed potato, making sure to fill all the way out to the edges of the dish You want to "seal" in the ingredients underneath or else they will dry out.

❖ Liberally sprinkle the pie with Asiago cheese and bake until heated through, about 30 minutes, depending on the thickness of the mashed potatoes and size of the casserole dish being used.

Caramelized Rib Eye Roast

From the Kitchen of Steve Loyer

Serves 6

Ingredients

1   **6-pound, bone-in Rib Eye roast**

3   **tablespoons Kosher salt**

2   **tablespoons fresh cracked pepper**

4   **large cloves garlic, crushed**

1   **cup honey**

❖ Preheat oven to 500° or your oven's highest temperature, but not on broil.

❖ Untie the rib eye roast and evenly distribute crushed garlic and a bit of salt into the folds. Re-tie the roast.

❖ Season roast evenly with pepper. Cover the entire roast with honey. Place the roast bone-side down in a shallow roasting pan. Insert a meat thermometer into center of roast.

❖ Place roast in hot oven and sear for 25 minutes. It will be smoking while the outside of the roast caramelizes. Reduce the heat to 300° and continue roasting about 1¾ to 2 hours for medium-rare (when thermometer registers 130° to 135°).

❖ Transfer roast to cutting board, loosely tent with foil and let rest 20 minutes. Slice and spoon pan sauce over each serving.

Sought after Ruby Beach, considered one of the crown jewels of the park, is named so because of the ruby-like crystals in the beach sand. Beach walkers and artists alike fall in love with Ruby.

Juniper Rubbed Venison Rib Chops with Huckleberry Semi-Glace

Chef Jess Owen, Ocean Crest Resort, Moclips

Serves 4

Ingredients

4   venison rib chops
    Salt and freshly ground
    pepper to taste
    Fresh ground Juniper berries
    to taste

Huckleberry Semi-Glace

1   tablespoon Olive Oil Blend
1   teaspoon Garlic
1½ tablespoons all-purpose flour
1   cup beef stock
½   cup huckleberries

Garnish

½   cup sliced green onions

❖ Prepare and heat a grill. Season venison rib chops and place on the grill. Cook venison, turning periodically until desired temperature is achieved. Remove from the grill and rest for 5 minutes turning over the meat halfway through the resting period.

❖ For the Huckleberry Semi-Glace, place a sauté pan on medium-high heat and add oil, garlic and flour. Stir garlic and flour until flour is fully emulsified, turning golden brown. Whisk in the beef stock and continue whisking until there are no lumps. Add huckleberries and bring to just under a boil. The sauce will tighten slightly. Remove from the heat and season to taste.

❖ When the venison is done resting and the Huckleberry Semi-Glace is ready, plate the venison, pour the sauce over the rib chops, and sprinkle with sliced green onions.

Olympic National Park, Oil, Troy Rohn

Filet Mignon with Blue Cheese Herb Crust

Serves 4

Ingredients

4   6 to 8-ounce filets mignons,
    tied, (about 1½-inches thick)

2   tablespoons olive oil
    Kosher salt
    Freshly ground pepper

For the Blue Cheese Herb Crust

½   cup fresh bread crumbs

¼   cup crumbled Blue cheese

¼   teaspoon dried rosemary

1   tablespoon minced,
    fresh Italian parsley

1   tablespoon minced,
    fresh chives

2   cloves garlic, minced

⅛   freshly ground pepper

❖ Preheat oven to broil.

❖ For the Blue Cheese Herb Crust, in a small bowl, combine all crust ingredients and mix well with a fork. Set aside.

❖ Season both sides of filets with salt and pepper. In a large skillet, heat oil over medium-high heat. Add filets and cook each side about 4 to 5 minutes, or to 120° to 130° for medium rare.

❖ Transfer filets to a baking sheet.

❖ Top each filet with an equal amount of crust mixture, packing the crust down on each filet.

❖ Broil the filets for 1 to 2 minutes or until the tops begin to brown.

❖ Remove from oven and serve.

Flat Iron Steak with Finnriver Habanero Cider Deglaze

Chef Dan Ratigan, The Fireside, Port Ludlow

Serves 4

Ingredients

4   8-ounce flat iron steaks

1½ teaspoons salt

¾ teaspoon black pepper

4   tablespoons Canola oil

1   medium shallot, cut into ⅛-inch dice

3   garlic cloves, finely chopped

8   ounces (give or take) Finnriver Habanero Cider

3   tablespoons demi-glace

❖ Pat steaks dry and sprinkle with 1 teaspoon salt and ½ teaspoon pepper.

❖ Heat 2 tablespoons oil in a 12-inch heavy skillet over moderately-high heat until hot, but not smoking. Cook steaks in two batches, turning over once, until meat is just medium-rare, 2 minutes per side. Transfer steaks to a platter as cooked and keep warm, loosely covered with foil. (Do not wipe skillet clean.)

❖ Add remaining 2 tablespoons oil to skillet and sauté shallot over medium-high heat, stirring, until shallot is golden, about 4 minutes. Add cider and cook until reduced to about ¼ cup. Add 3 tablespoons demi-glace, reduce heat and simmer about 3 more minutes.

❖ To serve, slice rested steaks on the bias across the grain. Top with sauce and enjoy.

The tide pools near Kalaloch and the surrounding beaches expose a rainbow of sea life. You'll find Sea stars, rock crabs, wolf eels, pricklebacks, brittle stars, barnacles, clams, sea snails and more.

La Push, Gouache, Mike Hernandez

Tomahawk Pork Chops with Bourbon Bacon Jam & Wine Poached Cranberries

Chef John Hermey, Ocean Crest Resort, Moclips

Serves 4

Wine Poached Cranberries

1 cup dried cranberries
1 cup white wine

Bourbon Bacon Jam

1 Pound Bacon diced
¼ white onion, diced
1 tablespoon chopped garlic
¼ cup Bourbon
⅓ cup Red Wine vinegar
⅓ cup Pure maple syrup
¼ cup brown sugar

Pork Chops

4 12-ounce bone-in pork chops
Salt and freshly ground pepper to taste

❖ For the Wine Poached Cranberries, place dried cranberries and white wine in a sauté pan on medium high heat. Bring to a boil and stir to fully hydrate cranberries. When nearly all liquid is absorbed, pour cranberries in a bowl and set aside.

❖ For the Bourbon Bacon Jam, render bacon on medium-high heat in a heavy bottom pot. Strain out the bacon fat and return bacon to the pot. Add the onion and garlic. Cook until the onion is softened. Remove from the heat and deglaze with Bourbon. In a safe area, ignite the alcohol with a grill lighter. USE CAUTION... There will be a fireball. Once the fire goes out, return the pot to the burner and add the brown sugar, maple syrup and vinegar. Cook until the liquid is a syrupy consistency. After cooling to around 120°, pulse Bacon Jam in a food processor until desired consistency is achieved.

❖ For the Pork Chops, season the chops to taste with salt and pepper and place on a medium-high grill. Cook the chops to desired doneness, turning occasionally to insure even cooking. Once the pork chops are ready, remove them from the grill and let rest for 5 minutes, turning half way through the resting period.

❖ For the final dish, heat Bourbon Bacon Jam in a pan and spoon a dollop onto a plate, place a pork chop on the jam and sprinkle Wine Poached Cranberries over the top.

Cider Braised Country Style Pork Ribs

Serves 6

Ingredients

2 pounds country-style pork ribs, trimmed of excess fat
  Salt and ground black pepper
1 teaspoon vegetable oil
4 slices bacon, chopped
1 medium yellow onion, chopped
1 large celery rib, finely chopped
6 medium garlic cloves, crushed
2 Golden Delicious apples, peeled, cored and sliced
¼ cup dried cranberries
3½ cups chicken broth
1 cup apple cider
2 tablespoons brown sugar
2 Bay leaves
2 tablespoons cornstarch mixed with 1 tablespoon water (cornstarch slurry)

❖ Adjust an oven rack to the lower-middle position and heat the oven to 300°.

❖ Pat the ribs dry with paper towels, season with salt and pepper. Heat the oil in a large oven-proof Dutch oven over medium-high heat. Place the ribs in a single layer and cook until well browned, about 6 minutes. Flip the ribs over and continue to cook until brown, about 4 minutes longer. Transfer the ribs to a plate.

❖ Pour off any fat remaining in the pot and return to medium heat. Add the bacon and cook about 3 minutes. Add the onion and celery and cook, stirring occasionally, until tender and golden brown, about 6 minutes. Add the garlic and cook 1 minute. Add apples, cranberries, broth, cider, bay leaves and browned ribs. Bring to a simmer. Cover, transfer to the oven and cook for 1 hour, until the meat is easily cut into.

❖ Transfer the meat with vegetables and fruit to a serving dish and discard Bay leaves. Heat the Dutch oven over medium heat. Add a small amount of corn starch slurry to the pan juices to thicken. Cook for 2 to 3 minutes, then pour the thickened juices over the ribs and serve.

Indian Fry Bread Tacos

Serves 6

Taco Filling

1   tablespoon vegetable oil
1   large yellow onion, diced
2   cloves garlic, minced
1   pound ground beef
1   packet Taco seasoning
¾   cup water
1   15-ounce can Pinto beans,
    drained and rinsed
1   7-ounce can diced, green chiles
    Salt and freshly ground
    pepper to taste
    Shredded cheese
    Shredded lettuce
    Diced Roma tomatoes
    Sliced black olives
    Sour Cream

Fry Bread

4½ cups flour
½   teaspoon salt
2   teaspoons baking powder
1½ cups water
½   cup milk
    Oil for frying
    (Safflower or Crisco)

❖ For the Taco Filling, heat oil in a large skillet over medium-high heat. Add onions and sauté 8 minutes until tender. Add garlic and sauté 1 minute.

❖ Transfer onions to a plate and add the ground beef to skillet. Cook the beef until browned and crumbled. Strain out the fat and add beef back to skillet. Add onions to beef.

❖ Stir in Taco seasoning and cook for 15 minutes. Add water, reduce heat and let simmer for 15 minutes. Add Pinto beans and green chiles and continue to simmer until liquid is absorbed. Season with salt and pepper to taste.

❖ For the Fry Bread, mix dry ingredients in a large bowl. Stir in the water and milk and knead several times.

❖ Make 6 balls from the dough and roll out into 6, 5-inch circles. Make a small hole in the center of each piece of dough with your fingers.

❖ In a large pot, heat several inches of oil to 375°. Fry the dough in batches and turn each when golden brown. Drain on paper towels

❖ To assemble the Tacos, spoon ground beef mixture into the center of each Fry Bread, top with cheese, lettuce, tomatoes, black olives, sour cream and serve.

Leg of Lamb with Yogurt-Cucumber-Mint Sauce

From the Kitchen of Michael Bloch

Serves 6

Ingredients

1   **5 to 7 pound leg of lamb, boned, butterflied and surface fat removed**

Marinade

½   **cup olive oil**

½   **cup dry red wine**

¼   **to ½ cup tightly packed, fresh mint, chopped**

6   **large cloves garlic, minced**

2   **Bay leaves, crumbled**
    Freshly ground pepper
    to taste

Yogurt-Cucumber-Mint Sauce

1   **cup Greek-style yogurt**

⅓   **cup finely chopped cucumber**

1   **teaspoon minced fresh mint**

2   **cloves of garlic, minced**

¼   **teaspoon freshly ground pepper**

1   **teaspoon White Balsamic vinegar**

❖ In a medium bowl, whisk together the Marinade ingredients. Pour into a large, resealable plastic bag. Add the lamb and set into a shallow container. Refrigerate for 24 hours, turning a few times.

❖ For the Yogurt-Cucumber-Mint Sauce, in a small bowl mix together all sauce ingredients. Cover and refrigerate for at least 4 hours before serving.

❖ About 30 minutes before grilling, remove the lamb from the Marinade and pat dry. Let the lamb rest and come somewhat close to room temperature. Discard the Marinade.

❖ Preheat a gas grill to high. Grill the lamb for 10 minutes on one side, then flip and grill for another 10 minutes. Reduce heat to low, lower the cover and grill another 40 minutes or until an instant read thermometer reads 125° to 130° in the thickest part for rare to medium-rare.

❖ Remove the lamb from the grill and let rest for 15 minutes before carving. Serve with Yogurt-Cucumber-Mint Sauce on the side.

Day or night, the rugged and wild coastline is a favorite place of artists.

Moon Above the Olympic Peninsula, Pastel, Heather Coen

POULTRY

Chicken Gnocchi

Sticky Chicken

Seared Duck Breast
with Wine Poached Cranberries

Oven Roasted Turkey Breast

Chicken Penne alla Vodka

Ginger Peach Chicken

Zesty Chicken Chimichurri

Curried Chicken & Butternut Squash

Northwest Waterfowl Stew

Sea Birds Cry, Silkscreen, Elton Bennett

Chicken Gnocchi

Chef Kaleb, Michael's Seafood & Steakhouse, Port Angeles

Serves 2

Ingredients

3   tablespoons olive oil
4   to 5 ounces raw bacon, diced
10   ounces chicken breast, diced
1   tablespoon minced shallots
1   tablespoon minced garlic
4   ounces white wine
4   ounces chicken stock
     (or canned chicken broth)
10   ounces heavy cream
6   ounces gnocchi dumplings
4   to 6 ounces Snow peas
½   ounce shredded Parmesan cheese
½   tablespoon minced, fresh
     Italian parsley
     Salt and freshly ground pepper
     to taste

❖ In a large skillet over medium-high heat sauté diced bacon until crisp. Remove from pan and set aside.

❖ Add chicken breast and lightly sauté for 1 minute without browning. Add shallots and garlic and sauté without browning.

❖ Add white wine and cook off alcohol. Reduce the liquid by 3-quarters. Add chicken stock and reduce by half. Add heavy cream, bring to a boil and reduce by half.

❖ Combine the bacon and remaining ingredients in the skillet, turn off heat, season to taste with salt and pepper and serve.

During low tide at Rialto Beach, visitors can access the tide pools, sea stacks, and the unique Hole-in-the-Wall rock formation. The surf can be pounding at high tide so careful planning is a must!

Sticky Chicken

Compliments of Wind Rose Cellars, Sequim

Serves 4

Ingredients

1 to 2 tablespoons olive oil

2 to 2½ pounds chicken (your selection of cuts or whole cut-up chicken)

1 to 2 cloves garlic, sliced

1 to 2 tablespoons fresh rosemary chopped (or tarragon, savory or thyme)

½ cup vinegar, diluted with an equal amount of water

❖ Heat olive oil in a heavy flat pan (such as a skillet) that will not crowd chicken. Brown chicken, turning to assure it browns on each side. Add garlic to pan and cook for few minutes. Add chopped herbs, stir to coat with oil, cook for about 1 minute.

❖ Pour vinegar mixture into pan and place lid, slightly askew on pan so liquid and steam can begin to evaporate.

❖ Simmer on medium-low heat for about 20 minutes.

❖ Turn heat up slightly and continue to cook until the liquid is completely evaporated and only a glaze is left in the bottom of the pan.

❖ Remove from heat and serve.

Seared Duck Breast with Wine Poached Cranberries

Chef Jess Owen, Ocean Crest Resort, Moclips

Serves 4

Wine Poached Cranberries

2   star anise
1   cinnamon stick
10 white peppercorns
10 black peppercorns
1   pound frozen cranberries
    Zest from 1 orange
    Juice from 1 orange
¼   cup red wine

Ingredients

4   duck breasts
    Salt and pepper to taste
½   cup Pure maple syrup

❖ For the Wine Poached Cranberries, make a spice sachet by placing the star anise, cinnamon, and peppercorns in cheesecloth and tying it closed. In a large non-reactive pot, combine spice sachet, cranberries, orange zest, orange juice and red wine. Cook on medium heat until cranberries just start to break down. Remove from heat and set aside.

❖ For the Duck, preheat oven to 425°. Score the duck skin and sprinkle with salt and pepper to taste. Place the duck in a large, cold pan, skin side down. Place the pan on medium-high heat until the skin turns a deep golden-brown color and fat is rendering in the pan. Turn over the duck breasts and sear the flesh side for 1 minute.

❖ Turn the duck breasts over again, skin side down, and place in the oven. Cook to desired doneness, approximately 6 minutes for medium-rare. Remove duck from pan and rest skin side up for 5 minutes. Keep the pan with the duck fat.

❖ For the sauce, place the pan of hot duck fat on a medium high burner. Add 1 cup of Wine Poached Cranberries and ½ cup of maple syrup. Stir to fully incorporate the sauce and remove from heat.

❖ To serve, place a large spoonful of the cranberry sauce on a plate and serve the duck breast on top, skin side up.

Wind Blown, Acrylic, Michael O'Toole

Oven Roasted Turkey Breast

Serves 6 to 8

Ingredients

1   6½ to 7 pounds whole, bone-in turkey breast with skin

3   tablespoons unsalted butter, softened

3   cloves garlic, pressed

1   tablespoon chopped fresh rosemary

1   teaspoon grated orange peel

1   teaspoon chopped fresh thyme

1¼ teaspoons Kosher salt

½   teaspoon freshly ground pepper

1   cup dry white wine or dry sherry

❖ Preheat the oven to 425°. Place the turkey breast on a greased rack in a roasting pan, skin side up.

❖ In a small bowl, combine the butter, garlic, rosemary, thyme, salt and pepper. Carefully loosen the skin from the turkey being careful not to break skin. With your hand, stuff some of the butter mixture under the skin as well as all over the outside of the turkey. Pour wine or sherry into the bottom of the roasting pan.

❖ Roast the turkey for 30 minutes. Reduce the temperature to 325° and continue roasting until the skin is golden brown and a thermometer inserted into the thickest part of the breast reads 160° (about 1 hour).

❖ When done, remove the turkey from oven to a carving board, cover with foil and let turkey rest at room temperature for 15 minutes.

❖ Slice the turkey breast, spoon juices from the pan over the slices and serve.

Chicken Penne alla Vodka

From the Kitchen of Jan Irwin

Serves 4

Marinara Sauce

2 28-ounce cans Plum tomatoes
8 large cloves garlic
2 large fresh, basil leaves

Ingredients

3 tablespoons unsalted butter
2 cloves garlic, minced
1 package sliced mushrooms
½ teaspoon red pepper flakes
½ cup vodka
1 cup heavy cream
4 pounds chicken tender fillets
4 eggs
1½ cups flour
   Salt and freshly ground
   pepper to taste
1 cup oil
1 pound Penne pasta

❖ For the Marinara Sauce, in a blender, pulsate all Marinara ingredients together. In a medium pot, bring the sauce to a boil then simmer on low for 1 hour. Set aside.

❖ Melt 3 tablespoons butter in a large non-stick skillet over medium-high heat. Add the mushrooms and sauté for several minutes. Add garlic and sauté 1 minute longer. Add the Marinara Sauce, red pepper flakes, vodka and cream to the skillet and bring to a boil, then reduce to a simmer. Season to taste with salt and pepper.

❖ For the chicken, crack the eggs into a bowl and whip until mixed. Place flour, salt and pepper in a separate bowl. Heat oil in a large skillet. The oil will be hot enough when a pinch of flour foams up immediately. Dip chicken fillets into egg, then flour, then back in egg mixture. Gently place in hot oil. Fry until brown on both sides and place on a paper towel covered platter to drain. Dip each piece of chicken in the Marinara Sauce, then keep chicken warm in a 170° oven.

❖ Cook the pasta according to package directions. Strain the cooked pasta and turn into a large pasta bowl. Add the Marinara Sauce to the pasta and toss. Top the pasta with cooked chicken and serve.

Rialto Beach, Watercolor, Jacqueline Tribble

Ginger Peach Chicken

Serves 4

Ingredients

2 tablespoons vegetable oil

4 skinless, boneless chicken breasts, pounded to an even thickness

½ teaspoon salt

¼ teaspoon freshly ground pepper

1 cup flour

⅓ cup milk

¼ teaspoon Cayenne pepper

2 tablespoons soy sauce

2 tablespoons rice vinegar

½ cup peach reserves

1 teaspoon freshly grated ginger

3 cloves garlic, minced

½ cup low-sodium chicken broth

4 large peaches, cut into ½-inch thick slices

Garnish

¼ cup fresh, chopped scallions

❖ In a shallow dish, combine the flour and Cayenne pepper and mix well. In another shallow dish pour the milk.

❖ Heat the oil in a large skillet over a medium-high heat.

❖ One at a time, dip each chicken piece in the milk, season with salt and pepper, dredge in the flour and then add to the hot skillet. Cook the chicken until browned, about 2 minutes per side.

❖ Meanwhile in a small bowl, combine the soy sauce, rice vinegar and peach preserves and set aside. When the chicken is browned, transfer to a plate and set aside.

❖ Add the ginger and garlic to the skillet and cook for 1 minute, stirring constantly. Add the chicken broth, the soy sauce mixture and fresh peaches to the pan. Turn the heat up to high and cook, uncovered, for about 5 minutes, stirring occasionally until the sauce is nicely thickened and the peaches soften. Add the chicken back to the skillet with the sauce, reduce heat to medium-low, cover and cook for about 5 minutes or until chicken is cooked through.

❖ Serve the chicken topped with the sauce and garnish with chopped scallions.

Sea Stacks are formed when powerful waves crashing against headlands erode the rock. Initially caves are formed. More waves create an arch, and when its center collapses, a sea stack is formed.

Zesty Chicken Chimichurri

Serves 6 to 8

Ingredients

2   pounds chicken drumsticks

Chimichurri Sauce

½   cilantro leaves

½   fresh Italian parsley

¼   fresh cilantro

3   tablespoons white Balsamic vinegar

½   teaspoon salt

½   teaspoon freshly ground pepper

2   cloves garlic, minced

1   teaspoon crushed red pepper flakes

¼   teaspoon cumin

½   cup olive oil

❖ For the Chimichurri Sauce, in a small food processor or blender, pulsate all sauce ingredients to a coarse puree.

❖ Pour all but ¼ cup of Chimichurri Sauce into a large, resealable plastic bag. Add the chicken legs, seal and set into a shallow container. Refrigerate for 24 hours, turning a few times.

❖ Preheat oven to 350°. Line a baking sheet with parchment paper.

❖ Remove marinaded chicken from the refrigerator 30 minutes before cooking to allow it to come close to room temperature. Arrange the chicken on the baking sheet and bake for 55 minutes or until done. Increase the oven temperature to broil. Broil for 2 to 3 minutes.

❖ Arrange the chicken legs on a serving platter, spoon the reserved Chimichurri Sauce over top and serve.

From Kalaloch Beach to Rialto Beach and further north, gray, orcas and humpback whales can be spotted, right from the shore.

Curried Chicken & Butternut Squash

From the Kitchen of Ronny Chirman

Serves 4

Ingredients

1½ to 2 pounds
butternut squash

1   pound boneless chicken
thighs or breasts

2   stalks lemon grass

1   red bell pepper,
cut into matchsticks

2   19-ounce cans coconut milk

4   to 6 tablespoons yellow
curry paste

2   tablespoons Palm sugar
(liquid if possible)

1   tablespoon fish sauce

1   to 2 tablespoons round turmeric

6   or more Kaffir lime leaves

1   cup basil leaves
(preferably Thai)

1   Jalapeño pepper, minced

1   juice of freshly squeezed lime

4   cups (or more) cooked rice

❖ Peel the squash and cut it in half. Remove seeds and cut into 1½-inch cubes.

❖ Cut the chicken into bite-sized pieces.

❖ Cut and save the bottom 5-inches of lemon grass stalk, discarding the rest. Split stalks in half lengthwise and hit with the flat of a knife to bruise.

❖ In a large pot, combine the lemon grass, coconut milk, curry paste, Palm sugar, fish sauce, turmeric, Kaffir leaves, basil and jalapeño. Mix well and bring to a simmer. Add chicken pieces and simmer for 15 minutes. Add the squash and bell pepper and simmer until just tender, being careful not to overcook it. Remove lemon grass stalks. Stir in lime juice and basil leaves.

❖ Divide cooked rice among 4 bowls. Ladle the Curried Chicken & Butternut Squash over each serving.

Northwest Waterfowl Stew

Compliments of Peninsula Sportsman Guide and Outfitting Service

Serves 4 to 6

Ingredients

2   large Canada goose breasts
     or 4 medium duck breasts
     (mallard, wigeon, sprig or scoter)

5   stalks celery

4   large carrots

1   medium white onion

12 to 15 small potatoes, Ozette
     or other fingerling potato,
     halved or quartered

2   cups sliced mushrooms (optional)

2   14.5 ounce cans stewed tomatoes

4   tablespoons corn starch

2   to 3 cups beef stock

1   packet onion soup mix

¼   cup fresh parsley

2   to 3 fresh rosemary sprigs
     Canola or avocado oil

1   cup flour

½   teaspoon garlic powder

½   teaspoon Sea salt

¼   teaspoon freshly ground
     black pepper

❖ Soak waterfowl breasts in saltwater (1 quart water to 1 cup Sea salt) overnight in the fridge to remove any excess blood or pellets in the meat.

❖ When ready to cook, rinse breasts thoroughly and pat dry. Cut meat into 1-inch pieces and dredge in flour mixture (flour, salt, garlic powder and black pepper).

❖ In small batches fry, duck/goose pieces in a large cast iron skillet with enough Canola or avocado oil to thoroughly coat bottom of pan, and slightly browning both sides of the meat.

❖ Remove the browned meat with tongs and place in the bottom of a medium to large crock pot. Cut carrots and celery and potatoes into 1" pieces, dice the onion and add together over the top of the meat. Add optional mushrooms and pour 2 cans stewed tomatoes on top. Add onion soup mix and corn starch to beef broth whisking thoroughly, then pour over entire mixture. (If you are adding mushrooms, using a little less water is preferred). Add fresh herbs.

❖ Cover and cook for 4 to 5 hours on high setting until tender.

An 8-mile round trip hike will take you to the stunning Point of Arches at Shi Shi Beach. Check the tides before you go!

Shi Shi Beach, Watercolor, Michael David Sorensen

VEGETARIAN

New Moon Fondue

Vegetable Chocolate Chili Mole

Chanterelle Mushroom Sauté

Potato, Leek & Chèvre Gratin

Roasted Beets, Sautéed Beet Greens
& Creamy Horseradish Sauce

Risotto with Red Onion, Parsley & Mushrooms

Mystery Bay Pizza

Grana Padana Crusted Ozette Potatoes

Wild Mushroom Bread Pudding

Lake Quinault Lodge, Digital Art, Laska Summers

New Moon Fondue

Compliments of Mt. Townsend Creamery, Port Townsend

Serves 4 to 6

Ingredients

1   bottle of dry white wine

1   clove garlic

1½ pound grated Mt. Townsend New Moon cheese

1   teaspoon dry mustard

2   tablespoons corn starch

     Ground pepper and nutmeg to taste

1   loaf crusty bread cut into cubes

     Various grilled meats and vegetables, cut into bite-sized pieces

❖ Rub the garlic on the inside of the fondue pot, then discard. Add wine, reserving two cups and turn on the burner. Heat slowly until bubbles form and slowly rise to the surface.

❖ Add corn starch and mustard to the grated cheese and toss. Add cheese to wine, stirring until smooth. Add reserved wine, if needed, if the fondue is too thick. Sprinkle with nutmeg and ground pepper to taste.

❖ Serve with accompaniments of your choice. Crusty bread, grilled meats, seared tomatoes, grilled peaches or raw vegetables. Enjoy!

Lake Quinault Lodge was built in 1926 and is located in the Olympic National Forest overlooking picturesque Lake Quinault. In 1937, President Franklin D. Roosevelt enjoyed lunch in the lodge's later-to-be-named Roosevelt Dining Room. Nine months after his visit, Roosevelt signed a bill creating Olympic National Park.

Vegetable Chocolate Chili Mole

Compliments of Olympic Cellars Winery, Port Angeles

Serves 6 to 8

Ingredients

3   tablespoons sesame oil

1   onion, diced

6   cloves garlic, minced

1   tablespoon course sea salt

½   cup vegan dark organic
    chocolate chips or chunks

1½ cups each: carrots
    and celery, chopped

1   each: green, red and yellow bell
    peppers, seeded and chopped

6   cups of any cooked beans

1   28-ounce can of diced tomatoes

1   cup corn kernels

2   Bay leaves

1   teaspoon each: thyme, ground
    cumin and basil

½   teaspoon each: cinnamon and
    chili flakes

⅛   teaspoon ground allspice

2   tablespoons chili powder
    Freshly ground black pepper

6   to 8 cups brown rice
    or Spelt Pita bread

❖ Heat oil in a large pot, add onions, garlic and sea salt. Cook until onions are translucent. Stir in the chocolate until it is melted. Add vegetables (carrots, celery, peppers) and beans and sauté for 5 to 10 minutes. Stir in the tomatoes and corn, reduce heat to simmer.

❖ Add Bay leaves, thyme, cumin, cinnamon, allspice, chili powder and several dashes of black pepper. Cover and simmer for about 30 minutes.

❖ Remove Bay leaves and serve with Spelt Pita bread or ladle over brown rice.

Chanterelle Mushroom Sauté

Chef Jess Owen, Ocean Crest Resort, Moclips

Serves 4

Ingredients

2	tablespoons olive oil blend
1	pound Chanterelle mushrooms
1	teaspoon chopped garlic
1	pinch Kosher salt
	Freshly ground pepper to taste
1	ounce white wine
1	tablespoon butter
1	tablespoon chopped parsley

❖ Place a large pan on medium-high heat and add oil. When oil begins to shimmer, add mushrooms, garlic, salt and pepper. Cook for 4 minutes stirring occasionally.

❖ Deglaze with white wine. Add butter, remove from heat and stir until butter is melted. Stir in parsley and serve.

The temperate rain forests found in the valleys of the Hoh, Queets and Quinault Rivers are found in only a few other places in the world. It's no wonder they are a national treasure!

Quinault River North, Oil, Kathryn Townsend

Potato, Leek & Chèvre Gratin

Compliments of Mystery Bay Farm, Marrowstone Island

Serves 4 to 6

Ingredients

1   tablespoon olive oil

4   large leeks, cleaned and thinly sliced (white and light green parts only)

5   garlic cloves crushed

2   cups of milk or half-and-half

3   tablespoons fresh thyme, plus more for garnish

8   ounces Mystery Bay Farm Chèvre cheese

1½ pounds Yukon gold or yellow Finn potatoes, thinly sliced

2   ounces (about ⅔ cup) grated Parmesan cheese
    Salt and freshly ground pepper to taste

❖ Preheat oven to 375° and lightly oil a 9 x 13-inch baking dish.

❖ Heat oil in a large skillet over medium-high heat. Add leeks and garlic. Sauté until leeks are tender.

❖ Spread one-third of the potatoes on the bottom of the baking dish, overlapping slightly. Sprinkle generously with salt, pepper and half of the thyme, then spread half of the leeks and crumble half of the chèvre. Repeat layering with potatoes, herbs, leeks and chèvre.

❖ Sprinkle over the last row (top row) of potatoes: salt, pepper and Parmesan cheese. Pour milk or half-and-half over the top. Cover with foil and bake for approximately 40 minutes (or until potatoes are tender). Uncover and bake 15 more minutes to lightly brown the top. Serve.

❖ Sprinkle with additional thyme before serving.

Roasted Beets, Sautéed Beet Greens & Creamy Horseradish Sauce

Compliments of Nourish, Sequim

Serves 4

Ingredients

3   pounds beets with greens

⅔   cup sour cream

3   tablespoons horseradish

½   teaspoon lemon zest

1   tablespoon minced chives

Salt and freshly ground pepper to taste

1   tablespoon butter

❖ Preheat oven to 350°.

❖ Cut greens from beets, reserving greens. Scrub and roast beets for at least 1½ hours, until tender. Cool, peel and slice beets into ¼-inch slices.

❖ Make the sauce by combining the sour cream, horseradish, lemon zest and chives. Add salt and pepper to taste.

❖ Wash greens well, chop stems into ¼-inch pieces and chop leaves into ribbons. In a sauté pan, melt the butter, add greens and cook for 3 to 4 minutes. Transfer to a platter.

❖ Sauté the cooked and sliced beets in a little butter until warmed through. Place on top of greens. Drizzle with horseradish sauce.

Near Lake Quinault, the Valley of the Giants is recognized by the National Forestry Association as having the largest living trees of their species.

Lake Quinault, Digital Art, Laska Summers

Risotto with Red Onion, Parsley & Mushrooms

Compliments of Wind Rose Cellars, Sequim

Serves 4

Ingredients

8   to 9 sliced mushrooms
    (Portabello, White Button
    or Shiitake)

1   medium red onion, chopped

1   large clove garlic, diced
    or thinly sliced

8   to 9 sprigs Italian Flat Leaf
    parsley leaves, diced, reserving
    1 tablespoon for garnish

4   tablespoons butter

1   tablespoon olive oil

⅓   cup dry red such as Wind
    Rose Cellars Bravo Rosso,
    or Barbera Columbia Valley

2   cups chicken or vegetable stock

1   cup Arborio rice, uncooked
    Salt and freshly ground pepper

¼   cup freshly grated
    Parmesan cheese

❖ Place broth in separate pan or microwave safe cup and heat. Meanwhile, sauté sliced mushrooms in heavy chef pan on medium- high heat until beginning to brown.

❖ Pour about 1 tablespoon of the wine over the mushrooms and let cook until wine evaporates (about 3 minutes). Remove mushrooms from pan and wipe pan.

❖ Add 2 tablespoons butter and 1 tablespoon olive oil to pan along with onion, diced parsley and garlic. Cook 2 to 3 minutes on medium heat until vegetables begin to brown.

❖ Pour rest of wine, about 3 tablespoons, into pan and cook until the wine is completely evaporated.

❖ Add 1 cup rice to vegetable mixture, stir to completely coat rice with buttered oil and sauté about 2 to 3 minutes. Stir continuously. Do not let rice brown.

❖ Add ¼ cup warmed broth to rice, stir into rice and cook until broth is completely incorporated. At this point, add the mushrooms back in to the mixture. Keep stirring for about 18 to 20 minutes, continuing to add broth, about ¼ to ⅓ cup each time, until the rice becomes tender but is still al dente. All of the broth should be absorbed but not dry. The rice should appear creamy.

❖ Remove from heat and add the remaining 2 tablespoons butter and Parmesan cheese, and mix together. Pour into a serving dish and garnish with parsley.

Mystery Bay Pizza

Compliments of Mystery Bay Farm, Marrowstone Island

Serves 4 to 6

Ingredients

Olive oil

Thin pizza crust

4 ounces Mystery Bay Farm Chèvre cheese, crumbled

Mild Italian sausage, cooked (optional)

½ teaspoon minced rosemary

½ cup sautéed shallots

❖ Spread thin layer of olive oil on pizza crust. Sprinkle Chèvre cheese, sausage, (if using) rosemary and shallots (and anything else that sounds good).

❖ Bake (follow your pizza crust recipe) until pizza crust is cooked through.

❖ Remove pizza from the oven, slice and serve.

The Quinault Loop Trail on the south side of the lake is one of the best trails on the Olympic Peninsula to see the beauty of a temperate rain forest.

Grana Padana Crusted Ozette Potatoes

Compliments of the Washington State Potato Commission

Serves 4

Ingredients

1   pound Ozette potatoes
    (fingerling potatoes)

4   cups vegetable oil

4   ounces shredded Grana
    Padana or Parmesan cheese

3   tablespoons extra-virgin
    olive oil

2   tablespoons cracked
    black pepper

2   tablespoons minced
    green onion

2   tablespoons minced garlic

2   tablespoons chopped Italian
    parsley

❖ Scrub potatoes with vegetable brush under cold running water. Cut in half lengthwise. Pat dry with paper towels.

❖ In cast iron skillet or large heavy saucepan over medium-high, heat the vegetable oil to 300°. Add dry potatoes in batches and cook until tender and golden brown, about 5 to 10 minutes.

❖ Drain on paper towels. In a large mixing bowl combine all remaining ingredients and stir to blend. Add potatoes and toss to coat. Serve hot.

Wild Mushroom Bread Pudding

Serves 6

Ingredients

3   tablespoons olive oil

6   ounces Shiitake mushrooms, stemmed and thickly sliced

6   ounces Oyster mushrooms, thickly sliced

6   ounces Cremini mushrooms, thickly sliced

2   Portabello mushrooms, stems and gills removed, thickly sliced

4   cloves garlic, chopped

1   tablespoon fresh basil, chopped

1   tablespoon fresh parsley, chopped

1   teaspoon dried sage

1   teaspoon dried thyme

5   large eggs

2   cups whipping cream

1   cup whole milk

¼   cup freshly grated Parmesan cheese, plus 2 tablespoons

¾   cup Gruyère cheese

¾   teaspoon salt

½   teaspoon ground pepper

6   cups crustless day-old dry white bread, cut in 1-inch cubes

❖ Preheat oven to 350°.

❖ Lightly butter 8 x 8 x 2-inch glass baking dish.

❖ Heat oil in heavy large pot over medium-high heat.

❖ Add all mushrooms, garlic, basil, parsley, sage and thyme and sauté until mushrooms are tender and brown, about 15 minutes. Remove pot from heat. Season mixture to taste with salt and pepper.

❖ Whisk eggs, cream, milk, ¼ cup Parmesan, Gruyère cheese, salt and pepper in large bowl to blend.

❖ Add bread cubes; toss to coat. Let stand 15 minutes.

❖ Stir in mushroom mixture.

❖ Transfer to prepared dish. Sprinkle 2 tablespoons cheese over. Bake until pudding is brown and puffed, and set in center, about 1 hour. Serve warm.

Painted on the chimney at Lake Quinault Lodge is a colorful totem pole-shaped rain gauge that measures rainfall in feet. The area receives an astonishing average of 131 inches of precipitation per year!

Rain Gauge, Digital Art, Laska Summers

DESSERTS & DRINKS

Lemon Berry Posset

Almond Carrot Cake

Twisted Strawberry Shortcakes
with Maple Balsamic Whipped Cream

Finnriver Pear Cake

Lavender Blue Ice Cream

Marionberry Cobbler

Chocolate Martini

Finnriver Sparkling Sangria Blanca

The Perfect Storm

Northwest Sunlight, Watercolor, Jacqueline Tribble

Lemon Berry Posset

Chef Ashley Miller, Creekside Restaurant, Kalaloch Lodge, Olympic National Park

Serves 8

Ingredients

4½ cups whipping cream

1½ cups sugar

½ cup, plus ⅛ cup freshly squeezed lemon juice

1 cup blueberries and blackberries combined

❖ In a large saucepan, combine the cream and sugar to a boil over medium-high heat. Boil for 3 minutes, stirring constantly. Do not over boil.

❖ Remove pan from heat. Stir in lemon juice and let cool for 10 minutes, then stir again.

❖ Divide the Posset evenly among dessert bowls or ramekins. Cover each serving with plastic wrap and refrigerate at least 4 hours or overnight.

❖ Top each Posset with an equal amount of berries and serve.

The park holds 650 archaeological sites, including one site, Ozette, which is eligible for National Historic Landmark status. Additionally, the park contains 130 historic structures and nearly 500,000 museum objects.

Almond Carrot Cake

Compliments of Nourish, Sequim

Serves 8

Ingredients

12 ounces fresh carrots,
    peeled and finely grated

6   ounces cane sugar

8   ounces pure ground
    almond meal

2   teaspoons baking powder

2   free range eggs, lightly beaten

2   ounces sliced almonds, toasted

❖ Preheat oven to 350°.

❖ Grease an 8-inch spring-form pan and line the base with parchment paper.

❖ Place carrots and sugar in a bowl. Add the almond meal and baking powder, stirring until combined. Mix in the eggs. Pour into prepared pan.

❖ Bake the cake for 45 to 50 minutes until center is firm. Remove from oven and sprinkle toasted, sliced almonds on the top.

❖ To serve, cut into 8 slices, top each with fresh whipped cream and grated carrots. And don't forget the Nourish signature decor, a fresh carrot top! Enjoy!

Twisted Strawberry Shortcakes with Maple Balsamic Whipped Cream

Chef Jess Owen, Ocean Crest Resort, Moclips

Serves 4

Ingredients

1   pound sliced strawberries
¼   cup sugar
1   teaspoon vanilla extract
3   teaspoons lemon zest, divided
2   tablespoons freshly squeezed lemon juice, divided
⅓   cup heavy cream
1   cup all-purpose flour
¼   cup sugar
1   teaspoon baking powder
¼   teaspoon salt
3   tablespoons cold butter, cubed
1   large egg yolk
¾   cup heavy cream
¼   cup Pure maple syrup
2   tablespoons Balsamic vinegar

❖ For the berries, in a mixing bowl, combine strawberries, sugar, vanilla extract, 1½ teaspoons lemon zest, and 1 tablespoon lemon juice. Stir together and set aside.

❖ For the shortcakes, preheat oven to 450°. Combine ⅓ cup heavy cream with 1 tablespoon lemon juice and set aside. In a large mixing bowl combine flour, sugar, baking powder and salt. Cut in cold butter until the mixture resembles crumbs. Add the egg yolk to your resting heavy cream and blend well. Add egg mixture to flour mixture and stir with a fork until just moistened. Do NOT over mix the dough. Turn dough out onto a lightly floured surface and gently kneed 4 times. Divide dough into 4 equal parts and pat each portion into a ¾-inch thick circle. Place your shortcakes onto a parchment paper lined cookie sheet at least 2 inches apart and place in the oven. Bake 8 to 10 minutes until golden brown. Remove from oven and transfer to a cooling rack.

❖ For the whipped cream, in a mixing bowl or stand mixer, beat ¾ cup heavy cream until it starts to thicken. Slowly add in ¼ cup Pure maple syrup and 2 tablespoons Balsamic vinegar. Stop mixing when medium peaks form.

❖ To bring it together, split open a shortcake and place on individual dessert plates, spoon over strawberries and top with Maple Balsamic Whipped Cream.

Dosewallips River, Oil, Kathryn Townsend

Finnriver Pear Cake

Compliments of Finnriver Farm & Cidery, Chimacum

Serves 4 to 6

Ingredients

2	cups flour
2	cups sugar
2	teaspoons baking soda
	Dash of salt
1	teaspoon ground cardamom
¼	teaspoon cinnamon
¼	teaspoon nutmeg
2	teaspoons vanilla
½	cup canola oil
2	eggs, beaten
4	cups diced or grated pears
1	cup floured nuts (optional)

Whipped Cream

½	cup heavy whipping cream
1	tablespoon sugar
1½	teaspoon Finnriver Pear Wine with Apple Brandy
	Dash of freshly ground nutmeg for garnish

❖ Preheat oven to 350°. In a large bowl, combine the flour, sugar, baking soda, salt, cardamom, cinnamon and nutmeg. Mix well.

❖ Add the vanilla, oil, eggs, pears and optional nuts to the dry ingredients. Mix well.

❖ Pour batter into a 9 x 14-inch pan and bake for 45 minutes. You may use 2 smaller pans and bake them for 30 to 35 minutes.

❖ Test the center of the cake for doneness as juiciness of pears varies.

❖ For the Whipped Cream, in a small bowl whip together the heavy whipping cream, sugar and pear wine until it holds soft peaks.

❖ Top each serving of cake with dollop of whipped cream and garnish with a dash of freshly ground nutmeg.

Lavender Blue Ice Cream

Serves 8

Ingredients

2   cups heavy cream
1   cup whole milk
½   cup mild honey
2   tablespoons dried edible lavender flowers
1   cup crushed fresh blueberries
2   large eggs
⅛   teaspoon salt

❖ In a medium saucepan, add the cream, milk, honey, lavender and blueberries. Slowly bring to a boil over medium heat, stirring occasionally. Once it begins to boil, remove saucepan from heat. Cover and let the lavender steep for 30 minutes.

❖ Strain the cream mixture through a fine-mesh sieve into a bowl. Discard the lavender and blueberry skins. Wipe out the saucepan and return the mixture to cook (do not simmer or boil) over medium heat.

❖ In a large bowl, whisk together eggs and salt. Slowly whisk in 1 cup of the hot cream mixture. Whisk in the remaining hot cream mixture into the saucepan and cook over medium-low heat, stirring constantly. Cook until the mixture is thick enough to coat back of spoon and reads 170° to 175° on a candy thermometer, about 5 minutes. Do not let boil.

❖ Strain the custard again through a fine-mesh sieve into a large bowl and cool. Cover and chill for 4 hours or overnight.

❖ Freeze custard in ice cream maker according to the manufacturer's instructions. Transfer ice cream to an airtight container and place in freezer to firm up.

Lake Quinault, Ink and Pastel, Marty Harris

Marionberry Cobbler

Roosevelt Dining, Lake Quinault Lodge, Quinault

Serves 12

Ingredients

1   gallon of fresh or thawed Marionberries

1   zest and juice of an orange separated

1   zest and juice of a lemon separated

½   tablespoon vanilla extract

¼   cup slurry (cornstarch and water)

¾   cup granulated sugar

Cobbler Topping

2   cups quick or instant oats

1   cup honey

❖ Preheat oven to 350°.

❖ Add the berries, orange juice, lemon juice and vanilla to a stock pot. Slowly bring to a boil, stirring occasionally. Whisk in the orange zest, lemon zest, sugar and cornstarch slurry. Allow to boil for three minutes to desired thickness, then cool and set aside. Pour berry filling into a large baking dish.

❖ For the Cobbler Topping, mix oats and honey together in a large bowl until well incorporated. Crumble mixture onto cobbler.

❖ Bake in the oven until top is golden brown and cobbler is bubbly about 35 to 45 minutes.

There are over 3,000 miles of alluring rivers and streams, 16 developed campgrounds and 611 miles of trails to explore in Olympic National Park.

Chocolate Martini

From the Kitchen of Ronny Chirman

Serves 1

Ingredients
1½ ounces chocolate liquor
1½ ounces Creme de Cocoa liquor
1½ ounces half and half
1   ounce vanilla vodka

Garnish
Chocolate syrup

❖ Drizzle a swirl of chocolate syrup around the inside of a martini glass for garnish. Chill in the freezer.

❖ In a cocktail shaker, add all ingredients and shake with ice. Strain liquid into the chilled martini glass and serve.

Full of life, Olympic National Park has 20 reptile and amphibian species, 37 native fish species, 300 bird species, and 56 mammal species, including 24 marine mammal species. The park is also home to the largest unmanaged herd of Roosevelt elk in the Pacific Northwest.

Finnriver Sparkling Sangria Blanca

Compliments of Finnriver Farm & Cidery

Makes 1 Pitcher

Ingredients

1   bottle of white or rose wine
1½ cups local fruit of your choice
3   cups frozen blueberries
2   cups Finnriver Sparkling Cider
    Add lemon, mint, sweetener
    and/or other fruits (optional)

❖ Pour wine over fruit and berries in a large punch bowl. Cover and let sit covered for 24 hours. Chill.

❖ Add Finnriver cider just before serving to maintain effervescence.

❖ Garnish each glass with additional berries.

The Perfect Storm

Compliments of Bedford's Sodas, Port Angeles

Serves 1

Ingredients

1½ ounces Grand Marnier

½ ounce freshly squeezed lime juice

3 ounces Bedford's Ginger Beer

3 drops Angostura Bitters

Garnish

Lime wedge

❖ Combine Grand Marnier, lime juice and bitters in a mixing glass.

❖ Add ice and shake vigorously. Strain over fresh ice into a highball glass, top with Bedford's Ginger Beer and swirl.

❖ Garnish with a lime wedge.

Visitors from all over the world come to Olympic National Park to enjoy and explore its monumental beauty that stretches from the mountains through the forest to the sea!

Forest Finds, Digital Art, Laska Summers

ARTISTS

COVER ARTIST
BARBARA BENEDETTI NEWTON

Barbara Benedetti Newton attended Burnley School of Professional Art (now renamed Art Institute of Seattle) and in 1965 began her professional art career as a fashion illustrator. Many years later, after several life changing events, Barbara co-authored *Colored Pencil Solution Book*, published in 2000. For the next decade soft pastel became her primary medium for impressionistic landscapes. In 2013, Newton authored the book *Art Answers: Pastel Drawing.*

Barbara is a Charter Member and past president of Colored Pencil Society of America; a Signature Member of the Pastel Society of the West Coast, Pastel Society of America and Puget Sound Group of Northwest Artists. Barbara is an International Association of Pastel Artists Master Circle Honoree and a Distinguished Pastelist in the Northwest Pastel Society as well as a Life Member Honoree of Women Painters of Washington.

Barbara is represented by Attic Gallery, Camas, WA, American Art Company, Tacoma, WA, and Scott Milo Gallery, Anacortes. She has been with Daily Paintworks selling work online since 2011. Her work is in collections worldwide. Barbara mentors artists through private sessions at her Black Diamond Studio. Visit: www.barbarabenedettinewton.com

ARTISTS

INTRODUCTION ARTIST
ELTON BENNETT (1910 - 1974)

Elton Bennett was born into a working class family in a town that sits on the very edge of the west coast of the continental United States. It is an area with unsurpassed natural beauty, home of the Olympic National Park.

Elton Bennett attended the Portland Art Museum School of Fine Art immediately following World War II. His first attempt at studying art had been derailed by the onset of the Great Depression, and there were long, hard years of manual labor long, before a glimmer of the dream could be rekindled. But those years provided the context for his silkscreen work- scenes of the working riverfront, the bustle of the commerce of the wharves, and his unflagging dedication to providing artwork to people of every economic class. His tenure at The Portland Art Museum School opened new vistas and, most importantly, introduced him to the Silkscreen/Serigraph printing process. Finally, he had found the way to create unique and constantly evolving artwork while maintaining his absolute belief in providing affordable artwork.

His silkscreen art portrays his beloved Pacific Northwest. His signature style of expressionistic realism speaks to those who relish the fog and mists of our beaches, the glory days of the 4 mast lumber schooners, and the tranquility of the forests.

Elton Bennett shunned the elitism of the establishment art world, deliberately placing his art in locations where people would never expect to find exquisite art; hardware stores, tackle shops, paint stores, stationery shops. Even occasionally at the local sandwich lunch counter. Visit: www.eltonbennett.com

ARTISTS

DAVID MCEOWN

Canadian artist David McEown has used the medium of watercolour for the past 25 years to explore and express many of this earth's disappearing wilderness areas. His paintings from Antarctica to the North Pole are represented in collections worldwide.

David is a graduate of the Ontario College of Art and Design and is an elected member of the Canadian Society of Painters in Watercolour, which in 2005 awarded him the society's prestigious A.J. Casson Medal. He also is a sought after teacher and has conducted workshops and multimedia presentations for numerous art societies and museums, sharing his reverence for nature and passion for the creative act of painting. When not sketching penguins down south or filming grizzly bears in Alaska, David can be found painting among the lush mosses of the Pacific Spirit Park along side his home in Vancouver, BC.
Visit: www.davidmceown.com

BHAVANI KRISHNAN

Bhavani was born in Switzerland in 1984. She spent her formative years in India and was always interested in art. After pursuing a career in engineering, she picked up the brush again in 2012 and rediscovered her passion for art. Since then she has participated and won awards in several plein air shows including Paint the Peninsula, Washington County Plein Air, Pacific Northwest Plein Air and Glacier National Park Plein Air. Her work is held in collections across USA, Europe and South America. Visit:
instagram@bhavanikrishnan
www.facebook.com/bhavaniKrishnanFineArt
www.bhavanikrishnan.com.
www.etsy.com/shop/BhavaniKrishnanArt

ARTISTS

KATHRYN TOWNSEND

I paint landscape, figure, portrait and still life, both in the studio and outdoor on location. My intent is to capture the varied harmonies of nature expressed not as picture stories, but as the visual and emotional relationship of shape and color. Painting is visceral. The paint itself, its color, texture and thickness, as it is laid on by brush or palette knife in the shapes of the abstract design, is how the story is told. From my studio window I am witness to the patterns and rhythms of the seasons, the tides and the wildlife of Zangle Cove on Puget Sound.

I have participated in painting exhibitions across the Country since 1989, including the Art in Embassies Program, most recently having paintings selected by the Ambassador to Jordan. Visit: kath.townsend@gmail.com
www.kathryntownsend.com
www.kathryntownsend.blogspot

LASKA SUMMERS

Laska Summers is a native of the Northwest who enjoys photography and creating digital art. Her passions are road trips, exploring nature and taking in the various culinary adventures the Northwest offers. Laska can be contacted through the publisher at beautyandbounty@outlook.com.

ARTISTS

ANDREW WICKLUND

Andy to family members, Drew to pretty much everyone else—he's happiest with a pen in one hand and a beer in the other...preferably at an outdoor cafe or trekking in an unexplored corner of the globe.

Drew works by day as a graphic designer and brand strategist, and does the occasional illustration job. You can occasionally find his artwork in a cafe or gallery, but most reliably on his Instagram page: @idrew365.

His first book, *I Drew People*, will be available in early 2018.

JACQUELINE TRIBBLE

Jacqueline Tribble is a Pacific Northwest watercolor artist specializing in dynamic landscape compositions. She completed a Bachelor of Fine Arts in Painting from the University of Washington and has exhibited in several countries including England, Italy, and the US. Jacqueline's work has won numerous awards and can be found in private and public collections in the US and Europe.

Lately, the artist has been focusing on depicting the various moods and atmospheres of the unique Northwest landscape, paying close attention to color and perspective.
Visit: www.jacquelinetribble.com

ARTISTS

SANDY BYERS

MARK BOYLE

Winning First Place in the animal/wildlife category in Pastel Journal magazine's Pastel 100 competition is a tribute to Byers' skill in the medium of pastel. In 2004, she entered her first competition: The Pastel Journal's Pastel 100 Competition; she won two awards in that juried competition. Her award-winning art has been published in multiple issues since then. Byers continues to gain acceptance and win awards in a multitude of juried shows. Her works are published in numerous magazines and hardbound books. Although Byers has produced works in a variety of media, her focus is working with oils and pastels. Many of her landscape and seascape paintings include scenes from her local area on Whidbey Island, in Washington State. Byers is well known for her heartfelt and expressive paintings of animals and she is passionately dedicated to supporting animal welfare organizations.
Visit: www.SandyByers.com

Mark Boyle is a native of the Pacific Northwest who has spent his life extensively exploring remote corners of the Olympic Peninsula. His inspiration for new work is gathered most often while hiking and fishing these areas.

A graduate of the Burnley School of Art, Mark also studied under noted painters such as Jeremy Lipking, Daniel Gerhartz, Ned Mueller and others.

In 2005 & 2012 Boyle was commissioned by Alaska Airlines to design a signature design featuring a large King Salmon across the entire fuselage. It was dubbed "Salmon-thirty-Salmon," and considered by many as the most intricately painted airplane in the world.

Mark Boyle's work is held in many permanent art collections, including the Laumeister Collection, Woodson Art Museum, Evergreen Hospital, West Coast Paper Company and the Yellowstone National Park. Visit: www.MarkBoyle.com

ARTISTS

ELIZABETH HENDERSON

I developed my own style a long time ago. As a full-professor of architecture for 21 years, I was amazed at the different styles represented by the thousands of students from many countries. We could all paint the same thing in so many different ways. I did my undergraduate studies in Warsaw, Poland, and have my Masters degree from UCLA.

I worked as a chief architect in California for many years for Pacific Bay Corporation in California and won many first place awards in architectural contests. I also taught architecture at a University in Maryland. Additionally, I worked as an assistant designer for MGM studios in Los Angeles.

I have a variety of styles from whimsical jazz musicians to European landscape. I mainly use acrylic but also have a collection in watercolor. I can be commissioned to paint anything, nothing is impossible!
Visit: www.elizabethhendersonart.com

JANET HAMILTON

Janet Hamilton is a regionally known painter of the northwest landscape, whose award-winning work is characterized by a beautiful sense of color and atmosphere. Janet was given the title "Snohomish County Artist of the Year" in 2001, and has exhibited in many galleries. She has worked mainly in the tradition of "plein air" painting, absorbing the colors and structure of nature while composing them into her own form of expression. Janet now works more often in her studio, where she teaches and creates larger paintings in both oil and pastel.

Janet is a member of the Women Painters of Washington, the American Society of Marine Artists and a Signature member of the Northwest Pastel Society. Her work is collected internationally, and has been published in the *Best of America: Pastel Artists, Vol. ll* and the Pastel Journal magazine.
Visit: www.janethamilton.com

ARTISTS

ROY LOWRY

Graduating in Commercial Art from Spokane WA, Roy worked in Chicago as an illustrator for a national sign company achieving national recognition. Relocating to Spokane, Roy began to watercolor gaining notoriety at the annual Western Art Show. Moving to Alaska Roy backpacked the State and worked on a crab boat fishing out of Dutch Harbor. Roy located his studio in Whittier, AK preparing for shows in Anchorage and Fairbanks. Moving to Hawaii Roy began an 18 year career as textile designer and creative director for a well known tropical shirt manufacturer. In 2009, Roy relocated to Ocean Shores and began painting full-time, inspired by Grays Harbor's diverse landscape and wildlife. Roy works wet to wet in watercolor applying controlled design and realism to his subject. He exhibits in local galleries and teaches watercolor weekly and in workshops. He is Co-Founder of North Beach Artists Guild and The Gallery of Ocean Shores located in Ocean Shores, Washington."
Visit: www.roylowrywatercolors.com

JAMES GEDDES

James Geddes has explored many facets of art. James was always drawing during childhood and later studied Japanese landscape design and complex masonry earthen art. In 2009, James became interested in painting with pastels. The following year his work was as accepted into the Northwest Pastel Society International Exhibit. James has since become a signature member of NPS and was President of the organization from 2016-2018.

"I love exploring western art, landscape and portraiture. My wife, Nancy, and I still enjoy photographing the fall seasons and the dazzling colors. That is what we were doing when I took the reference photo for Hoh River Bend. We love the Olympic Peninsula and have returned many times!" Visit: www.jamesgeddespastels.com

ARTISTS

SHIRLEY MERCER

TROY ROHN

Shirley Mercer is a semi-realistic watercolor painter who is currently displaying at the Port Townsend Gallery in Port Townsend, WA. She is from Georgia, Florida and Alaska and makes her home in Sequim, WA. She also teaches watercolor at various locations, displays in local and national shows and runs a small graphic design and frame shop.

Her current projects include "A Story to Tell." Mercer says, "We all have a story...some past, some present and some haven't been written yet. Good stories of fun, fame and fortune, but also some dark moments that we'd rather forget. Our stories are made of major dramatic events and mere snippets of life barely remembered. As technology shrinks our world, we find our community—our tribe—expanding. Through the arts we can reach out to this expanded community. Our stories connect. Our stories intertwine. Our stories bridge our differences." Visit: www.shirleymercer.net or shirlmercer@gmail.com.

I am a neuroscientist by day and painter by night. I live, work, and paint in the beautiful state of Idaho and have spent much of my life in the Pacific Northwest and Montana. Many of these areas have served as inspirations for my art work. I have been painting in oils for about 8 years and probably inherited some painting genes from my dad, who was also an artist.
Visit: www.troyrohn.blogspot.com

ARTISTS

MIKE HERNANDEZ

A native Angeleno, Mike Hernandez is a plein air painter skilled in gouache, oil and acrylic, whose works have been featured in several on-line publications as well as galleries. His process began as a young child, painting still life images. Influenced by the likes of Edgar Payne, Sorolla and Franz Bischoff, Mike soon explored the foundations of color and light in the outdoors – striving to find the beauty in the ordinary. With a palette that resides at the crossroads between industrial and landscapes, he finds inspiration anywhere from the Eastern Sierra range to the muddy concrete banks of the Los Angeles River. Mike studied at Art Center College of Design in Pasadena, graduating with a B.A. in 1998. Currently, he is a Production Designer at Dreamworks Animation as well as a nation-wide sought-after workshop instructor. His works can be found in several private collections around the world. Visit: www.mikehernandez-art.com

HEATHER COEN

Juried into 30 national and international shows in the last 48 months, Heather has attained "Master Signature Circle" for Paint America, and has "Signature Membership" in The Pastel Society of Colorado and Plein Air Artists of Colorado. She was included in the prestigious "Plein Air Rockies" taking the Silver Award and Wyoming's "Prairies to Peaks" taking First place. Heather was juried into Women Artists of the West 45th Annual Show in Tucson, Arizona at the Desert Art Museum in November, 2015. A solo show at Boyce Thompson Arboretum State Park Gallery was held in August and September of 2014. She currently has work in four galleries in three states.

Heather lives in Gilbert, Arizona with her beloved basset hounds Mallory and Gus and her faithful husband, Richard. Visit: www.painthewild.com

ARTISTS

MICHAEL O'TOOLE

Michael's love for design led him to explore his creativity in variety of media including watercolour, pen and ink, graphite, gouache and acrylic. Currently focusing on acrylics, his diverse subject matter ranges from landscape and seascape, to architecture and portraiture. His travels both locally and internationally have also been a tremendous source of inspiration.

Michael's canvas prints are published by Canadian Art Prints and are sold in print Galleries around the world with much acclaimed success. Several magazines (Magazine Art , International Artist) newspapers and articles are always writing about his story and journey on the "Road Less Traveled," the life of a full time artist for over 20 successful years.

Michael's work may be found in thousands of corporate and private collections across Canada, USA, Europe and Japan.
Visit: www.otooleart.com

MICHAEL DAVID SORENSEN

Michael David Sorensen began watercolor painting at age 12. His love for art had begun several years earlier after hundreds of drawings attracted attention from peers. As a new painter, Michael was given a deadline that sped up his learning process: a directive from his father in early December the following year to paint and frame a painting as a gift for his grandparents, and have it wrapped and under the tree by Christmas Eve. With a non-negotiable deadline, he became a quick study in watercolor, and got the painting done just in time. Michael created more paintings as gifts for his grandparents, and fell in love with it along the way. His love for the beautiful surroundings in the Pacific Northwest encountered while hiking, camping and road tripping provided endless ideas for paintings. In time, Michael developed a distinctive style for outdoor scenes. Never one to shy away from taking creative license in his subjects, he frequently infuses imagination and bright colors into beloved scenes from around the Pacific Northwest and wherever else his travels take him.
Visit: www.etsy.com/shop/MichaelDavidSorensen

ARTISTS

MARTY HARRIS

Marty Harris is an Artist and Illustrator. He has been a digital illustrator for over thirty years, since receiving his MFA in painting from Indiana University Later sketchbooks became a passion. He founded an international sketchbook exchange, which at its height had 400 participants around the world. Marty began making prints while studying for his BFA at Tyler School of Art in Philadelphia. He picked up printmaking again in 2008, first at Highpoint Center for Printmaking, then at The Minneapolis College of Art and Design. Intaglio and screen printing are terrific media for the drawer and graphic artist. Marty and Vic began taking regular trips toward the North Shore of Lake Superior. They became particularly fond of the dramatic landscape of Jay Cooke State Park. In 2015, Marty was honored to work as an Artist-in-Residence at The Grand Marais Art Colony. Visit: www.martyharrisfineart.com

POINTS OF INTEREST

BEDFORD'S SODAS
Port Angeles WA 98363
www.bedfordssodas.com

CAMARADERIE CELLARS
334 Benson Road
Port Angeles WA 98363
360-417-3564
www.camaraderiecellars.com

**DOCKSIDE GRILL
ON SEQUIM BAY**
2577 West Sequim Bay Road
Sequim WA 98382
360-683-7510
www.docksidegrill-sequim.com

FINNRIVER FARM & CIDERY
124 Center Road
Chimacum WA 98325
360-339-8478
www.finnriver.com

**HAMMA HAMMA
OYSTER COMPANY**
35846 N US Hwy 101
Lilliwaup WA 98555
360-877-5811
www.hamahamaoysters.com

**KALALOCH LODGE
OLYMPIC NATIONAL PARK**
157151 Highway 101
Forks WA 98331
866-662-9969
www.thekalalochlodge.com

**LAKE CRESCENT LODGE
OLYMPIC NATIONAL PARK**
416 Lake Crescent Road
Olympic National Park WA 98363
888-896-3818
www.olympicnationalparks.com

LAKE QUINAULT LODGE
345 South Shore Road
Quinault WA 98575
888-896-3818
www.olympicnationalparks.com

**LOG CABIN RESORT
OLYMPIC NATIONAL PARK**
3183 East Beach Road
Port Angeles WA 98363
888-896-3818
www.olympicnationalparks.com

**MICHAELS SEAFOOD
& STEAKHOUSE**
117 B East 1st Street
Port Angeles WA 98362
360-417-6929
www.michaelsdining.com

MT. TOWNSEND CREAMERY
338 Sherman Street Port
Townsend WA 98368
360-379-0895
www.mttownsendcreamery.com

MYSTERY BAY FARM
Marrowstone Island WA 98358
360-385-3309
info@mysterybayfarm.com
www.mysterybayfarm.com

NOURISH
101 Provence View Lane
Sequim WA 98382
360-797-1480
http://www.nourishsequim.com

POINTS OF INTEREST

OCEAN CREST RESORT
4651 SR 109
Moclips WA 98562
800-684-8439
360-276-4465
www.oceancrestresort.com

OLYMPIC CELLARS WINERY
255410 Hwy 101
Port Angeles WA 98362
360-452-0160
www.olympiccellars.com

**PENINSULA SPORTSMAN
GUIDE AND OUTFITTING
SERVICE**
1280 Cape George Road
Port Townsend WA 98368
360-379-0906
www.peninsulasportsman.com

**SOL DUC HOT
SPRINGS RESORT
OLYMPIC NATIONAL PARK**
12076 Sol Duc Hot Springs Road
Port Angeles WA 98363
888-896-3818
www.olympicnationalparks.com

THE FIRESIDE
One Heron Rd
Port Ludlow WA 98365
360-437-7412
www.portludlowresort.com/the-fireside

**WESTPORT WINERY
GARDEN RESORT &
SEA GLASS GRILL**
1 South Arbor Road
Aberdeen WA 98520
360-648-2224
https://www.westportwinery.com

WIND ROSE CELLARS
143 W Washington
Sequim WA 98382
360-681-0690
www.windrosecellars.com

RECIPE INDEX

RESOURCES

- ❖ National Park Service - Olympic National Park
  www.nps.gov

- ❖ Olympic Culinary Loop
  www.olympicculinaryloop.com

- ❖ Wikipedia
  www.wickipedia.org

- ❖ www.recreation.gov

- ❖ www.olympicnationalparks.com

- ❖ www.myolympicpark.com

- ❖ www.thekalalochlodge.com

- ❖ Washington Potato Commission
  www.potatoes.com

- ❖ www.forkswa.com/listing/log-cabin-resort

- ❖ www.wta.org/go-hiking/hikes/marymere-falls